Once Upon a Time...

ONCE

The Early Years of the

LEONARD SHECTER

UPON A TIME...

New York Mets

Introduction by Maury Allen

The Dial Press
New York

Published by
The Dial Press
1 Dag Hammarskjold Plaza
New York, New York 10017

Lyrics on page 128: © 1962 Sunbeam Music, Inc. Used by
permission of copyright owner.
Some of the material on the 1962 New York Mets first
appeared in an article in *The New York Times Magazine*.

Copyright © 1969, 1970 by Leonard Shecter

All rights reserved.
Manufactured in the United States of America
First paperback printing

Library of Congress Cataloging in Publication Data
Shecter, Leonard.
Once upon a time—the early years of the New York Mets.
Previously published as: Once upon the Polo Grounds.
1970.
1. New York Mets (Baseball team)—History. I. Title.
GV875.N45S5   1983   796.357'64'097471   82-22045
ISBN 0-385-27930-2

*For Casey Stengel
Who made it all beautiful*

Introduction

Casey Stengel, a bowlegged, craggy-faced seventy-one-year-old gnome, stood in the back of an open truck rolling slowly down Manhattan's Seventh Avenue that Thanksgiving Day in 1961. His orange-colored hair blew in the stiff fall wind and his eyes teared from the cold. He wore no topcoat and his huge tie kept billowing over his shoulder from under his California-style sports jacket.

The old man, just a year after being ousted as the manager of the exalted New York Yankees, leaned over the top wooden rail of the moving truck to sign an autograph for a small boy. "Amazin'," said Stengel to the wide-eyed kid, "my Mets are gonna be amazin'."

And they were, mostly because of Stengel. On that afternoon one could easily see what the Mets would be about. They would be forever young—as their manager was—forever amazing, entertaining, exciting, rambunctious, amusing. They would be, as Stengel's descendants, the people's team.

As I recall my days as a young reporter watching the rebirth of New York National League baseball and the emergence of a new team, two things remain crystal clear in my memory about those early Mets.

One, of course, was Stengel.

Introduction

The other, maybe even more significant, was the skill, talent, wit, attitude, professionalism, and enthusiasm of a band of New York sportswriters. It was the sportswriters who put the Mets into print. It was this group of baseball historians who set the tone for a team that has never been equaled. The sportswriter for the *New York Post* was Leonard Shecter. He was my friend, colleague, and predecessor in covering the Mets, and was an invaluable teacher to me.

Shecter once watched a drunken Yankee pitcher named Ryne Duren squash a cigar in Ralph Houk's face on a brawling Yankee pennant train. Houk squashed Duren's face with his fist. Shecter's story caused both Duren and Houk to threaten him.

"The thing you got to remember," Shecter told this young reporter once, "is that you have to be there after you write a tough story."

He often described himself as a curmudgeon and said his motto was "Only kick a man when he is down." Shecter liked to think of himself as a tough guy.

But it was all an act. He was a lovable guy who showered much affection on Casey Stengel and the early Mets. Shecter kept his leukemia to himself and when he left us, well before anybody was ready, his funeral service evolved into an endless series of funny stories, many of which were about the Mets. They were about Gil Hodges and Marvelous Marv Throneberry, Stengel and boss George Weiss, owner Joan Payson and chairman M. Donald Grant. They were about long-lost treasures of Met lore: Butterball Botz, Dawes Hamilt, Ted Lepcio, and Sammy Drake.

Once Upon a Time: The Early Years of the New York Mets resurrects those lost treasures. There is the kid who came down to that first Met camp after throwing a few

Introduction

baseballs under the Triborough Bridge and deciding he could make the team. There is the veteran minor-league player named Rod Kanehl who was championed so courageously by Shecter that the first banner to ever fly in the Polo Grounds simply read: HOT ROD. And there is the husky slugger named Frank Thomas who always meant well. He meant so well that he used to walk through airplane aisles waking sleeping teammates to ask, "Gonna eat?" Reading these pages one can understand the anguish in an eighteen-year-old ballplayer's heart when he shows up at the Polo Grounds to see a sign reading: IS ED KRANEPOOL OVER THE HILL? Shecter is quick to remind Kranepool's tormentors that the young first baseman drew a full World Series share in 1969 and has a ring and a Series home run ball to prove it.

Like the first girl you love, the early Mets grow more beautiful with the passing days—Richie Ashburn, the white-haired right fielder; Choo Choo Coleman, who when asked if he knew his roommate's name responded, "Yeah, bub, you number four"; Gus Bell; Felix Mantilla; Roger Craig; and Don Zimmer. It was Stengel, as Shecter reported, who understood Zimmer's worth to the team. The ex-Dodger had gone thirty-four times without a base hit. When he finally singled, Stengel told Shecter, "I have to trade him while he's hot." In this delightful romp through the past Shecter makes the early Mets heroes come alive. These are the Mets that were, the Mets, for heaven's sake; players who would be the forerunners of (a few actually participants in) baseball's most miraculous title—the 1969 World Series Mets. No other expansion team, except for the 1982 Milwaukee Brewers, has ever won a pennant, and the Mets have won two. You could look it up.

Introduction

What makes this book such a joy is that marvelous relationship between the past and the present. Baseball teams have a history, some stretching back more than a hundred years, but no team ever was able to link its past with its present as well as the Mets. How else can we fully appreciate a four-hundred-foot home run by Dave Kingman in a 10–0 game and a strikeout in a 1–0 game to end it by the same guy called Kong if we do not truly understand the deeds of Frank Thomas, the Big Donkey? The turmoil surrounding poor Jay Hook, the craftiness of Al Jackson, and the toughness of Roger Craig needs to be understood before we can fully appreciate the conquests of Tom Seaver, Jerry Koosman, and Nolan Ryan. And don't forget that the Mets got a break on Opening Day of 1962 by being rained out, and were not touched again by such good fortune until they avoided playing fifty games in 1981 with a strike. All of that past is part of the present. No team has had so much fun, so much excitement, so much drama, surround them in all the history of sports.

It is hard to say whether the early Mets were special people. Stengel certainly was. But Marv Throneberry actually struck out a lot, had an iron glove, and swallowed his chewing tobacco too often. And yet it is Marvelous Marv who sells beer on television, not Ashburn, the .300 hitter, or Kranepool, who made it as a Series star, or Kanehl, the least talented, most productive Met of all.

We want it that way because we want to remember the Mets as they were. There will never be a team as ingloriously charming as the 1962 Mets or as lovingly improbable as the 1969 Mets. There will never be a team as horrendously unsteady as the 1973 Mets, who just about ended their season with a forty-two-year-old future Hall of Famer named Willie Mays falling down in the sun under

Introduction

a fly ball anybody—well, not a 1962 Met—could have caught.

More has been written and said about the Mets in their two decades than has been written about a dozen other teams with a century of history. I salute the editors of The Dial Press for bringing Shecter and the Mets back together in this wonderful look at the past.

Casey Stengel had an expression about some of his long-lost teammates. "A lot of people my age," he would say, "are dead at the present time." Through these pages the old Mets live again. And Casey is there with them. For a lot of us who remember, so is Leonard Shecter, who has chronicled that joyous time.

Maury Allen
January 1983

Once Upon a Time...

Year VIII

Preposterous. The idea that the New York Mets, the everloving New York *Mets* for goodness' sakes, for seven years laughed at and ridiculed, the team that was created a loser and seemed destined to be a loser forever, the idea that this misbegotten bunch of lovable incompetents would not only win a National League pennant but go on to humiliate the Baltimore Orioles, winners of 109 games in the American League, simply *annihilate* the Baltimore Orioles in the World Series was . . . well, simply preposterous.

We were, none of us, ever going to be old enough to see a day like this. Our lot was to be forever enveloped in a cult of sweet misery, the kind enjoyed for so many years when the Brooklyn Dodgers were "Dem Bums." The Mets made music to lose by, to love hopelessly by, to reminisce by. But there was never going to be that hot, thumping rhythm of a march to the pennant and a world championship. Not for us. For our sons, perhaps, or their sons.

Think of it this way. The Pittsburgh Pirates have been nine years without a pennant, the Philadelphia Phillies nineteen, the poor Chicago Cubs twenty-four. So there is only one explanation for this thing that happened in

Leonard Shecter

1969, Year VIII of the New York Mets. There are those who believe that the explanation is that life *does* follow art and that Douglass Wallop knew something when he wrote *The Year the Yankees Lost the Pennant,* that someone indeed had sold his soul to the devil. Leo Durocher, the manager of the Chicago Cubs, could have felt that, and a lot of other baseball people who watched the Mets and said, "I see it, but I don't believe it." Only there are no devils, not anymore, anyway, and those of us who were there at the beginning, those of us who watched the Mets day after ironic day, who saw them bobble away games through nothing more than happenstance and ill luck, we know what happened. It was this: *Seven years of terrible luck evened out in a single season.*

Everyone in baseball knows the rule. You get some bad breaks, you get some good breaks. They even out. Except that for seven years the Mets got only bad breaks. They really did. We thought, most of us, that they were unlucky because they were bad. It was the other way around. For no one could have been as bad as the Mets. No team in history ever lost 737 baseball games in only seven years, no team ever attracted such calamity, lost so often that it became funny. Defeat in baseball is supposed to be grim. With the Mets it was hilarious.

Then it all turned around. In one season the Mets got all the breaks, made all the catches, squeezed winning hits out of .215 hitters like the last toothpaste from a tube, grabbed every break by the throat and wrung it dry.

People knew. They made jokes about it, but they knew. Something eerie was happening. Like during the World Series someone asked Tom Seaver, the pitcher (if there *was* a pact with the devil Seaver was Shoeless Joe Hardy), if he thought God was a Met.

Once Upon a Time . . .

"No," he said. "But I think he has an apartment in New York."

The Mets were good. As Willie Mays was to say over the winter, "People ask me what the Mets did right, and I say, 'What did they do wrong?' " But there were few teams in the league who would have been willing to swap lineups with the Mets at the beginning of the season. There are *still* few teams that would. Certainly not the Baltimore Orioles, and all the Mets did to *them* was beat them four out of five.

Where did it start? Can we tell, with the advantage of our shiningly clear hindsight, where it turned? Is there a place we can put a finger and say here, this is where good luck and Mets became synonymous?

How about this. The Mets got Tom Seaver, 25-game winner, Cy Young Award winner, in a raffle. Yes they did. While he was still in college he signed a $50,000 bonus contract with the then Milwaukee Braves. It turned out, though, that the Braves had violated baseball rules by signing him after the season had started. So he was raffled off. The Mets won.

That was in 1965. So it must have started then. Not on the field, of course; in 1965 the Mets lost 112 games, only eight fewer than they'd lost in 1962, the first and grandest year of them all. On the field, it all happened in 1969. It not only happened that the Mets played well, that their fly balls dropped for hits, that they made superhuman defensive plays, it happened that there seemed to be what Casey Stengel, the One Great Met, called a "whommy" on the opposition. A "whommy" is Stengelese for whammy, or hex. A whommy is when a pitcher strikes out nineteen Mets and loses, which is what happened to Steve Carlton of the St. Louis Cardinals. He broke a

Leonard Shecter

record for strikeouts and was defeated by two home runs by Ron Swoboda. It was a fantastic event, yet hardly noticed, for it was just another day in the life of the new, lucky Mets.

There were others. There was the first game of the first crucial series in Met history, the one game that, more than any other, signaled the mysterious collapse of the Chicago Cubs. The Mets won it when a young Cub outfielder named Don Young, in the game more for his glove than anything else, let one ball fall in front of him for a double and gave up another two bases when he bounced off the fence and allowed the baseball to dribble out of his glove.

Losing a game, one game in a season of 162, couldn't make all that difference. Except that this game so bugged the Cubs, Durocher especially, that it wound up as trauma. Like what can you do about a kid that blows a ball game? Pat him on the tail, see if you can give him a lift, save his psyche for another day. But what did Leo Durocher, one of the great managers of our time, do? He said the kid should have caught both those fly balls, easy. He said the kid was a disgrace. He said it loud. He said it in public.

So did Ron Santo, the third baseman. Santo later apologized. Durocher never did. It sat with the Cubs— and the rest of the league for that matter—like wiener schnitzel for breakfast. There is evidence that at that precise moment Durocher no longer had the confidence, much less the loyalty, of his players.

Besides, there was this ninth-inning situation in that game. The winning run was on second, first base was open and Ed Kranepool, a hot Met hitter, was the batter. It was possible to walk him. Durocher elected to pitch to

Once Upon a Time . . .

him. Kranepool threw his bat at an outside pitch and plunked it into left field for the winning hit. The last time Kranepool hit the ball to left field Leo Durocher was a nice guy. Take that, Lady Luck.

And when Durocher was asked why he didn't walk Kranepool, he didn't rant, he didn't rave, he didn't roar. He just got up and walked out of the room. The Lip had been buttoned.

Then there was the game with the Cubs in which an umpire's decision helped the Mets win. It didn't use to happen that way. Quite the reverse, of course. First there was a vital hit by Bud Harrelson. You have to understand about Harrelson. Early in the season he weighed in at about 165. By this time he was down to 145 and fading fast. His strength was as less than one, which was exactly right for the way he hit the ball. If he hit it any harder it would have been caught. In the old days of the Mets, Harrelson would have lost not an ounce and hit the ball firmly, right at somebody. As it was, no one could handle it as it flopped around the infield like a flounder out of water. This set the stage for Tommy Agee to unload a two-run homer.

A good thing, too, because Jerry Koosman, the Met pitcher, allowed the Cubs to tie the score in the sixth. In the bottom of the sixth Tommy Agee hit what should have been a single past third base. He had no business trying for two and if he had been an old Met he would have been thrown out from here to there. Instead, he so astonished the Cub left fielder that the man just stood there, gaping instead of throwing. Agee made second easily.

From there he scored on Wayne Garrett's single. That is, the umpire said he scored. Leo Durocher said he

Leonard Shecter

didn't score, and Randy Hundley, the Cub catcher, leaped so high in protest there are eyewitnesses who swear it took him two minutes to come down. In fact, it did look as though Hundley's sweeping tag had caught Agee. But the umpire's decision stuck, of course, just as it always used to when the calls were going against the Mets.

There's more, lots more. You can't win thirty-eight of forty-nine games in the last weeks of a season if the breaks are evening out. No way—*unless they've already been evened out.*

How about the time Al Weis, the glove man, hit his first home run of the year. It came just in time to knock in three runs against the Cubs. The next day, the Mets won again because Al Weis hit *another* home run. In almost seven years in the major leagues, this skinny thirty-one-year-old man with an "s" missing from his name had hit a grand total of four (4). And what about the Mets winning twelve of fourteen games against the rough, tough west, or taking a nine-and-a-half-game Cub lead in August and turning it into an eight-and-a-half-game Mets lead in September? When the Giants did less in 1951 they called it a miracle.

Then there was the playoff against Atlanta. This was the first year of the new playoff system and there was an extra mountain to climb. The Mets didn't bother climbing it. They just kicked it over. The way they treated Henry Aaron and Orlando Cepeda and the Atlanta Braves was a caution.

If before the first game you had told the Braves that they would score five runs against Tom Seaver, the best pitcher in North America and all the other continents, they would have smiled happily and started counting

Once Upon a Time . . .

their World Series shares. In fact they *did* score five runs off Seaver, but they didn't win because the Mets scored nine runs off Phil Niekro, the knuckleball man. The Mets' big inning was the eighth, an inning in which Orlando Cepeda threw a ball in the general direction of home plate and hit the ground in front of him instead, as though the ball were made of something sticky, like flypaper, an inning in which the reliable Tony Gonzales destroyed a baseball in center field, an inning in which the Mets ran around the bases the way people used to run around against them. It was a wondrous sight. They scored five runs. You had to keep checking your scorecard to see who was in the field. You kept thinking it had to be the Mets.

The Mets won the second game 11–6 after compiling a 9–1 lead. The Braves never had a chance. They made three errors that somehow managed to look like ten. So someone asked Clete Boyer, the third baseman, if he thought tension was telling on the Braves. "I don't know," he said. "But I'll say this. These are different ball games than you play in the summer."

Maybe so, but the Mets didn't seem to notice.

Back in New York, the third game was simple. All it required was a managerial move of such eerie prescience that Casey Stengel himself was thunderstruck. It happened in the third. The Mets were down 2–0 and young Gary Gentry was struggling on the mound. Tony Gonzales led off with a single. Henry Aaron, who had hit a two-run homer in the first, rapped a double to left. This brought up Rico Carty. With the count one and one Carty slammed a pitch hard on a line to left field that seemed certain destiny to deliver three runs. At the last moment, though, the ball curved foul.

Leonard Shecter

Then Hodges made his move. You don't see many managers remove a pitcher with the count one ball and two strikes on the hitter. Said Casey Stengel: "I took a lot of fellows out with the Mets, but all *those* balls were hit fair."

Hodges' move worked. Of course. Nolan Ryan came in throwing blue darts. He struck Carty out. Said Paul Richards, the astute, florid, simmering general manager of the Braves, "Nobody else on the Mets' staff could have done that to Carty."

Cepeda was then purposely walked and Ryan struck out Clete Boyer. The third out was a routine fly ball. The Mets went on to win by a score of 7–4. "After that," said Richards, "I believe the Mets could win anywhere, including Vietnam."

They didn't have to win in Vietnam, only against Baltimore. It was easy. The whommy always makes it easy.

The Mets lost the first game of the Series because Brooks Robinson, the Baltimore third baseman with the three hands, took away their big offensive weapon, the infield roller. They'd been doing great with it all season, scoring runs because they weren't hitting baseballs hard enough to break a pane of glass. Robinson, though, barehanded them to death in the first game of the series by a score of 4–1, even beating Seaver in the process. "If the infield grounder is their best shot," said the round manager of the Orioles, Earl Weaver, "they're in trouble—because we got the best infield in baseball."

After that Agee, a brilliant outfielder, and Ron Swoboda, who wasn't quite, made historic catches, Al Weis flexed his bony arms and hit yet another home run, Rod Gaspar, the symbol of Met anonymity ("Bring on Rod Gaspar," the Orioles had shouted in derision before

Once Upon a Time . . .

the Series), made an enormous impression and, at the end, the best infield in baseball made the errors that turned the Mets, the New York *Mets,* for heaven's sake, into World Champions.

Al Weis, the .215 hitter, knocked in the winner in the ninth as the Mets won the second game, 2–1. After the third game, won by the Mets, 5–0, people were walking up to Frank Robinson of the Orioles and asking him if he had become a believer of what was now obvious to one and all—that the Mets were the chosen people. "When I see them fly," Frank Robinson said, "I'll believe it." Then he added, "Have you seen them fly?"

Well, yes. Tommy Agee was seen to hit a home run in the first inning and then he was seen to make two incredible catches in center field with a total of five runners on base, all of whom would have scored with anything less than this brilliance. And then pitcher Gary Gentry, who was 0 for 38 going in, was seen to knock in two big runs with a double in the second and well, yes. The Mets *did* fly.

Especially Agee. With two on in the fourth Elrod Hendricks of the Orioles hit a ball deep to center that was slicing toward left. After a long chase during which time seemed to hang in the air along with the ball, Agee stuck out his glove, backhanded, and the ball fell into it. There was still time to drop it, though, the way, say, Don Young did that fateful day. A lot of white showed in the webbing of Agee's glove as he got a bare hold, bounced off the wall and, at last, held it. It wasn't until then that it was noticed that nobody in the jam-packed ball park had been breathing.

In the seventh, the Mets were leading by four runs, but the bases were loaded when Paul Blair crashed a drive—into right center this time. Where it was sup-

Leonard Shecter

posed to say "National League" on the baseball, it said "Triple." Sometimes that happens with a baseball.

Except Agee got on his horse again and ran, and ran, and when he saw he couldn't catch up to the ball he dove, just at the conjunction of green grass and red-clay track. To the surprise of the multitude, and probably of the ball, Agee slipped his glove under it just as it was about to make a nice big bounce off the track. It was the kind of catch nobody in New York had seen since Willie Mays was a colt.

Agee thought the first catch was toughest. Gil Hodges thought the second was. And Baltimore Manager Earl Weaver said that by his count seven runs scored in the process. Five maybe, but seven? "Sure," he said. "Those runs score, don't you think Hendricks and Blair score too?"

Sure. And if the Orioles could score seven phantom runs, the Mets could fly. Frank Robinson probably knew it all the time.

The debate over which of Agee's catches was the best ever seen in a World Series was still raging the next day when Ron Swoboda settled it all by making one of the dumb-great catches of all time. Tom Seaver, pitching better at last, was beating the Orioles 1–0 going into the ninth. Then Frank Robinson and Boog Powell singled. Brooks Robinson followed with a low line drive to right field which any intelligent fielder would have played on one hop, sacrificing a run, but at least making sure the ball didn't go by him, which would allow *two* runs to score. Except Ron Swoboda doesn't think that clearly, not when he's wearing a baseball suit, anyway. He never thought for a moment of protecting the Mets, the score, or himself. He went after the baseball, the way a bulldog goes after the seat of the pants. He

Once Upon a Time ...

galloped in and to his right as fast as he could, stuck out his hand, fell down, slid on his belly and made the catch.

It couldn't be done. In some alternate world that ball went by him to the fence, two runs scored, the Series was tied at two games each, and the Orioles went on to win it in six. But in this world, the place where nothing bad could happen to the Mets anymore, Ron Swoboda made the catch.

A run scored, tying the game. But that was all. And in the tenth, the Mets unleashed Rod Gaspar. The play, as Ron Swoboda described it later, looked like a Chinese fire drill. It was totally recognizable to Mets fans who had watched the Mets blow dozens of games through the years, just that way. Only this time it happened to the Baltimore Orioles.

Jerry Grote of the Mets led off with what should have been an ordinary fly ball to left. Except Don Buford, a good outfielder, picked the ball up late, broke back toward the fence and then had to turn around, run in and let the ball bounce in front of him. Grote reached second, and Gaspar ran for him. The mighty Al Weis was purposely walked and J. C. Martin, batting for Seaver, put down a routine bunt. At best, all it should have done was advance the runners. But Pete Richert, the pitcher, somehow managed to pick the ball up, throw it toward first base *and hit Martin on his wrist.* Even that wasn't whommy enough. Instead of just dropping to the ground and allowing the Orioles to deal with a bases loaded situation, the ball bounced nearly all the way to second base while Oriole infielders chased it and Mets ran around the bases like Swoboda's Chinese fire drill. In the confusion, Bring On Rod Gaspar scored the winner. The next day photos of the action showed that

Leonard Shecter

Martin should have been called out for interference. He had run outside of the base path and having been hit there was palpably guilty. Except for one thing. Nobody noticed. Not Weaver, not the Orioles, not the umpires.

After that, there was no question about who was going to win the next game. Of course Frank Robinson *was* hit in the groin by a pitched ball. He had a bruise this big to prove it, and the World Series movie confirmed it all. Yet the ump blew it, he blew a call in favor of the Mets again. And Robinson didn't reach base.

In the bottom half of the same inning the ump was about to blow another. He said Cleon Jones had not been hit in the foot. So Gil Hodges strode majestically out of the dugout, ball in hand, to show the shoe polish on it. This time the Mets *proved* the umpire wrong. So then it was certain that Al Weis *(Al Weis?)* would hit a home run to tie it up and that the Orioles would make two more errors and that the Mets would win, 5–3. Game, set, and match.

The fans tore up the Shea Stadium turf and in downtown New York there was a spectacular, spontaneous, unrehearsed outpouring of ticker tape and other paper that took days to clean up. It was a day when people in New York City smiled at each other.

However, the most moving thing said about the Mets had been said the day they clinched the pennant. George Weiss, the elderly retired president of the Mets, stuck his head into Gil Hodges' crowded office, smiled his tight little smile and said, "Nineteen-sixty-two."

Hodges grinned a big-toothed grin. His eyes shone with amused understanding. "Nineteen-sixty-two," he said.

That was the year the Mets started paying their dues.

Year 1

It is difficult to think of New York as a ghost town. When the Brooklyn Dodgers and the New York Giants, baseball traditions in the city since 1900, deserted to the west coast in 1958, the city went on. There were shows on Broadway and off, none of the museums shut down, restaurants flourished, the rentals on midtown apartments kept going up. Yet there was indeed something missing. New York was not a ghost town as our cousins in the west were saying, but an *excitement* was gone, the excitement of National League baseball.

In those days, before expansion and the decline of the New York Yankees homogenized baseball, the Yankees dominated the American League, and the only question each season was on what date they would clinch the pennant. There was a good deal of what Casey Stengel called brother-in-law baseball in the American League. Let's not anybody here get hurt. What was the use? The Yankees were going to win anyway.

In the National League it seemed to get more difficult each year to predict a pennant winner. Races went down to the wire. Often there had to be playoffs. Each game was important and there was a lot of biting, kicking, and scratching in the games. National League teams worked

Leonard Shecter

for their runs. They stole and hit and run and bunted and squeezed. In the American League everybody sat around waiting for somebody to hit a home run, the way the Yankees always did it. But then the Yankees always had someone to do it.

Even National League fans were different from American League fans. The crowds at Yankee Stadium were always quieter, better dressed, and knew less about the game than the fans at Ebbets Field and the Polo Grounds. There was nothing to match the crowds who came to Dodger-Giant games. Noisy, tough, knowledgeable, the fans themselves became part of the show. The heroes were bigger than life. Mel Ott, Bobby Thomson, Willie Mays, Jackie Robinson, Duke Snider, Roy Campanella, Carl Furillo, Pee Wee Reese. Just reciting the names still brings a prickle to the back of one's neck.

And suddenly they were gone. All at once. All of them. In 1957 they played their schedules in New York. We all knew by then that they were leaving, yet none of us believed until the following year when they left spring training and went home—not to New York, but to California.

Those who cared very deeply would take the train down to Philadelphia when the Dodgers and Giants came in. Clumps of New Yorkers sat in the stands for these games and booed their old heroes.

In New York, meanwhile, there were those who hadn't given up. With the constant urging of New York sportswriters as a spur, plots grew to bring National League baseball back to New York. The best of them was not really a plot at all, but a genuine attempt to form a third major league. Branch Rickey, who brought Brooklyn from the cellar to the dome of the National League, was the guiding force behind this attempt. He believed that

Once Upon a Time . . .

a new league could start off with what amounted to minor league talent, but that since competition would be keen, the low level of talent wouldn't matter. In that manner, he believed, the new league, which was to be called the Continental, could slowly grow to maturity and compete on an even basis with the two established leagues.

It was a good theory, so good that it could be used as a bludgeon, particularly since people with real money were rushing in to grab Continental League franchises. Organized baseball was no longer playing with kids; the threat was real. In New York the money belonged to Mrs. Charles Shipman Payson, who was a long-time stockholder in the Giants. She has money she still hasn't counted. With her was William A. Shea, a lawyer and dabbler in city politics. Shea, a bluff, hearty man with a ready smile, a loud voice, a sneaky-fast backslap, and a hair-trigger mind, saw very quickly that he could frighten organized baseball with the Continental League. He did it so well that in 1961 the American League expanded to ten teams, and a year later, so did the National. The Continental League was dead. But the New York Mets had been born.

From the beginning everything about the Mets was like something seen in a funhouse mirror. Nothing was what it appeared to be and every time anybody took a firm position he turned out to be standing on a banana peel. For example, shortly before the Mets came into some shimmering form of reality, journalist Jimmy Cannon wrote in the New York *Journal American,* "The type of team the Mets assemble will decide whether Casey Stengel manages them or remains in the banking business. The old Yankee manager, who is stalling George

Leonard Shecter

Weiss, president of New York's new National League franchise, would be agreeable to a one-year contract if he believes he has a respectable team to run. Otherwise, the Journal American was informed, he will remain out of baseball forever."

Then we have the matter of the National League trying to get the two new clubs—Houston was also being inducted into the League—to pay maximum money for minimum talent. No bones were made that the purchase of talent was actually a price of admission. And what did the franchise actually cost Mrs. Joan Shipman Payson, one of the wealthiest women in the world? Why a terrible $1,800,000. Thousands were outraged at the holdup. Now, only eight years and one pennant later, the Mets, if available, would bring a minimum of $12,000,000 in the marketplace. You've got to admire the National League owners for that. They really put it to that gullible Mrs. Payson.

The NL owners were a lot more successful in stiffing Mrs. Payson with what was laughingly called talent. The first Mets were has-beens, never-weres, and you-paid-$125,000-for-who? Cloaking themselves in honesty, civic virtue, and the American flag, the NL moguls conspired to leave their expansion rosters nude of young talent. In the years since that first draft George Weiss has often been blamed for choosing overage destroyers (that is, as old as the destroyers the United States sent Britain in 1940) and dooming the Mets to less than mediocrity for years to come. That was true enough. Weiss did indeed think he needed big-name players in order to induce the foolish multitudes to pay their way into the ancient and decrepit Polo Grounds (whose ancientness and decrepitude he tried and failed to cover with whitewash). He was

Once Upon a Time . . .

wrong. Yet he hadn't much choice. Overage destroyers had been thrust upon the Mets—and the Houston club. In fact the outspoken Paul Richards, who headed the Houston organization, announced to a group of newspapermen after he had seen what was available to him in the draft, "Gentlemen, we're fucked."
And Richards was also wrong. For a mere million-eight Houston had started the Astrodome dynasty—worth more these days than the wildest dreams Judge Roy Hofheinz, the owner, has in his baroque mezzanine bedroom.

When Casey Stengel agreed to manage the Mets, on September 29, 1961, he leaned back into the deep swivel chair in the office of his bank in North Hollywood, California, and talked about how happy he was to be running the New York Knickerbockers. It was a half hour at least before he realized they were the Mets. And a week at least before he began calling them amazing.
Casey's next mistake was in not showing up at the big expansion draft meeting in Cincinnati. The reason he didn't, he explained abashedly, was that he had guessed wrong about the World Series. The draft was to take place in the city in which the Series ended. Stengel and nearly everybody else expected the Yankees and Cincinnati Reds to have to come back to New York to finish up, but the Yankees swept in Cincinnati and won the Series 4 games to 1.

Roster of Honor, the twenty-two original Mets:
Craig Anderson—At twenty-three years old, Craig Anderson was an underage destroyer. He won 4 and lost 3 with the St. Louis Cardinals in 1961, his first season in

the major leagues. This was, it turned out, his best year.

Gus Bell—In 1953 Bell hit 30 home runs for the Cincinnati Reds. During his best years his batting average hovered between .280 and .308. In the year before he got to the Mets his average dropped to .255 and he hit only 3 home runs. That's why the Mets got him. That and because he was thirty-three years old. And because, some guessed correctly, he was through.

Ed Bouchee—In his first year with the Philadelphia Phillies Bouchee hit .293. That was in 1957. It was his best year.

Chris Cannizzaro—In 1969 Chris Cannizzaro had a pretty good year with the San Diego Padres.

Elio Chacon—Cincinnati had a terrible World Series against the Yankees in 1961 but Elio Chacon had a good one. He seemed quick, exciting, and very able. It turned out he was quick and exciting.

Choo Choo Coleman—As a part-time catcher with the Philadelphia Phillies in 1961, Choo Choo hit .128.

Roger Craig—A nice man and a pretty good pitcher, Roger Craig deserved a better fate. Losing 24 games for the Mets in 1962 left marks on him that are still visible.

Joe Christopher—He hit .263 for the Pirates in 1961, his first full year in the major leagues. One wondered why the Pirates gave up on him. The answer soon became obvious. He was a terrible fielder. Still, he's a Met Hall of Famer. He played 154 games for them in 1964 and hit .300.

Ray Daviault—At age twenty-seven Ray Daviault was still a minor-league pitcher.

John DeMerit—He had a big year with the Milwaukee Braves in 1961. He hit .162. It wasn't for nothing that he was called "Thumper."

Sammy Drake—A bright lively chap who sat on the

Once Upon a Time . . .

bench for the Cubs in 1961. That was the year in which he did not get a single base hit.

Jim Hickman—For years Jim Hickman was one of the Mets' best players. They didn't go anywhere until they got rid of him.

Gil Hodges—This man was delivered as damaged goods. He never did a thing for the Mets.

Jay Hook—A keen student of the game and a promising pitcher, Jay Hook was always a keen student for the Mets.

Alvin Jackson—He was twenty-five years old at the time and had been in the Pittsburgh organization since 1955. They were wrong to get rid of him. Probably the best pitcher to go in the expansion draft.

Sherman "Roadblock" Jones—He once said, "I only believe 12 percent of what I read in the newspapers." He was a better philosopher than he was a pitcher.

Hobie Landrith—Thirty-one-year-old catcher who looked twenty-eight and played like forty. Hobie always said he was 5-8. He probably was 5-6. It wasn't his fault he wasn't big enough to play this game.

Felix Mantilla—This was a fellow who seemed to have a lot of talent. But he never liked to play baseball.

Bob Miller—He was an in-and-out right-handed pitcher for the St. Louis Cardinals. Between 1957 and 1961 he compiled a 9–9 record. In 1962 he won one game for the Mets and lost 12. Possibly as a reward during that humbling season, the Mets obtained another Bob Miller, Robert G. Miller (as opposed to righty Robert L.). Robert G. won two games for the Mets, but the big thing was that the Millers shared a hotel room and when the phone rang either one could pick it up and say, "Bob Miller here."

Bobby Gene Smith—Who? Bobby Gene Smith, that's

who. Seven years in the major leagues. Right-handed-hitting outfielder. Lifetime average: .243. Batted .136 in an eight-game career with the Mets.

Lee Walls—This original Met was never an original Met. He was traded in December of 1961 along with a hundred thousand dollars to the Los Angeles Dodgers for second baseman Charley Neal. The Mets had paid $175,000 for Walls. It can safely be said that Charley Neal was not a $275,000 second baseman.

Don Zimmer—By the time Don Zimmer got to the Mets all he had left was his hustle.

These are some of the things that George Weiss had to say after the player draft:

"Records weren't the only means which guided us in our selections. All of these players were thoroughly scouted and their potentialities were weighed as much as their current records."

Also: "A year ago the selections made by Los Angeles and Washington as they came into the American League were not too prepossessing at first. But, as it turned out, quite a few unknown quantities revealed themselves as excellent players upon being given the chance to play regularly."

And: "Our major aim had been to get men of experience. And while there now remains a tremendous lot of work to be done, I honestly believe we have the nucleus around which we can build an interesting ball club."

Not long after, Weiss managed to wrest Frank Thomas away from the Milwaukee Braves for a mere $125,000.

Thomas, who didn't mind being called Big Donkey, was thirty-two years old, but had hit .281 and 27 home runs for the Milwaukee Braves in 1961. At the time of the

Once Upon a Time . . .

deal it was believed (1) that Lou Perini, the owner of the Braves and a construction millionaire, was trying to do something nice for Weiss; (2) that the bottom had fallen out of the construction business; or (3) George Weiss knew how to hypnotize people. It turned out the answer was (4) Perini knew Frank Thomas.

Still, Stengel seemed delighted by the whole thing. "We got men like Thomas, Bell, Hodges, Walls, and Zimmer," he said. "We're going to hit the ball out of the Polo Grounds once in a while."

And they did, once in a while.

Before their first season began, the Mets accomplished what the New York Yankees could not do in thirty years—they integrated St. Petersburg, Florida. St. Pete, long the home of the Yankees in spring training, was not exactly a Deep South town, but Negro ballplayers on the St. Louis Cardinals and Yankee teams could not stay at the same hotels as the rest of the players. The Yankees had moved out of St. Pete, hinting darkly that segregation was one of the reasons. In fact they were making themselves what they counted as a better deal in Fort Lauderdale. Proof is that in the same year the Yankees departed the Mets and Cards both found motels that would accept Negro players, the Mets at a place on the Gulf of Mexico, the Cards on the causeway heading south.

But the Mets weren't able to go all the way. The personality of George Weiss was such that he always held back something. He was a stiff, cold man who brought with him from his days with the Yankees an unfriendliness that might have destroyed the good will which fell so easily to the Mets, had it not been for his old friend

Leonard Shecter

Casey Stengel. One of the great wonders of the world is that Stengel and Weiss were able to remain friends through the years. Perhaps it was that they were such different men.

In any case, although the team and the press were comfortably ensconced at a beach motel, Weiss insisted that the club headquarters remain at the old Soreno Hotel. There was a certain charm to this crumbling old establishment, a charm personified by live chamber-music concerts in the lobby. But it was this hotel which had, for so many years, so steadfastly refused to allow Negro ballplayers to live there.

For the Mets to continue to use the Soreno as their office and press headquarters was a triumph in reverse public relations. The new Met organization had a mind-bending knack for this kind of coup.

An example was their choice of a public-relations man. The fellow Weiss hired was the late Tom Meany. Now Meany, newspaper man, author, raconteur, was widely respected in his field. He was the original Joe Garagiola. He could entertain a barroom full of people into ridiculous hours of the morning. The one thing he couldn't do was run a baseball club's public relations department. It simply wasn't part of his personality, his view of life, or of himself. It is the job of public-relations men to help other people, often with quite nitty-gritty tasks. Meany was willing only to amuse them.

One time a *New York Times* man asked Meany for a press brochure. "Press brochure?" Meany said. "I haven't got enough of them for myself." And he strode off in a huff.

The stiff-backed George Weiss, the crotchety Tom Meany, the absent Mrs. Payson (who spent most of her

Once Upon a Time . . .

time in Europe or at the race track)—none of them mattered. They didn't matter because Casey Stengel was, without seeming to try, the best public-relations man a baseball team could have. When the Mets arrived in St. Petersburg it was obvious that Casey Stengel had already taken over the town. A banner stretched across the main street read "WELCOME N. Y. METS AND CASEY STENGEL." The motel where the Mets were to live had a huge picture of the old man out front: "HOME OF THE NEW YORK METS AND CASEY STENGEL." Inside, at the desk, there was an engraved sign: "STENGELESE SPOKEN HERE."

St. Petersburg, a town of old people, identified with Stengel. His accomplishments at age seventy-one brought a warm glow to the elderly inhabitants. As far as they were concerned, Stengel *was* the Mets.

At a department store in St. Pete, where Stengel was autographing copies of his book, *Casey at the Bat*, which was the story of his life in baseball, or part of it anyway, the customers were white-haired, most of them, and some needed canes to support them. All spoke a few words with Stengel, recalled old days, came away grinning, eyes sparkling. One lady, who had put down $3.95 for the book, set a jar of preserves carefully wrapped in aluminum foil in front of Stengel. "I want you to have it," she said to him. Stengel's mobil face creased into a wide grin.

"They're calamander preserves from my orchard," the gray-haired lady said gently to a reporter nearby. "I figured everybody takes from him and I wanted to give him something."

Everywhere he went crowds gathered. People applauded. Reporters wore their pencils down to nubs. What could have been dull, even ludicrous, routine, a battered bunch of outcasts like the Mets trying to get ready to play in the same league as Willie Mays, took on

Leonard Shecter

a glitter of special interest. As long as Casey Stengel was there the Mets were big league.

In his first speech to his players Casey Stengel said, "Spend carefully, take your shoes off when you come into the clubhouse, and play good."

Lunch that first day in the clubhouse was hot soup, cold hard-boiled eggs, carrot slices, and celery, just like what Ralph Houk ordered for the Yankees when they trained there. Stengel used to be a bread-and-cold-cuts man when he managed the Yankees, but he was perfectly willing to change. "Why should I be old-fashioned, just because I'm old?" he said.

At the end of the day Stengel posed for pictures with Mrs. Payson. "We're gonna win some games," he said. "We're not poor people."

It was that first day, too, when it became evident that Casey Stengel was not going to get along with his coach Rogers Hornsby. You could tell, because Hornsby wore his baseball spikes into the clubhouse and scattered mud all over the carpet.

From that first day Casey Stengel set out to prove the Yankees had been wrong to fire him. The energy of this old man, who had been accused of falling asleep on the Yankee bench (the Yankees were so efficient they could put a whole ball park to sleep), was fantastic. He started right off showing people how to bunt without squaring off the Rogers Hornsby way. "If you do that, everybody knows you're going to bunt," Stengel explained.

He also found time that day to put a little knock in on Ralph Houk of the Yankees. "That fella said I hollered at the players too much," Stengel said, "but I notice he's playing the players I hollered at."

Once Upon a Time . . .

Because of Stengel, because of what the Mets represented in the hearts of their countrymen in New York—the return, at last, of National League baseball—this spring of 1962 was a season of hope. Since hope is an inexpensive commodity, it was spread around the Mets generously.

The kid's name was John Pappas. He was skinny, 5-10, not more than 150 pounds, and the sallow pallor of the city was on his face. He had a lot of black hair which he was wearing in a scraggly pompadour as he walked into the clubhouse of the Mets in St. Pete that February morning, plunked down his little canvas bag with the well-worn sneakers and tattered baseball glove inside, and announced he was a pitcher and ready. The funny thing was, nobody laughed.

It couldn't happen now. He was a twenty-one-year-old unemployed furniture salesman from Queens who had never thrown a baseball for an organized team. "Just some PAL stuff," he said. "Also stickball, like Willie Mays." Today he'd be seized, stuffed into a straitjacket, and whisked away to the nearest head hospital. Then, at that time and place, however, he was handled gently. Who had ever told him, he was asked, that he could be a big leaguer? "I told myself," John Pappas said. "I'm not exactly a Herb Score, but I'm pretty fast." He stuck out his skinny, unimpressive chest.

The historical fact is that the Mets actually took a look. Johnny Murphy, then assistant to George Weiss, wasn't altogether happy about it. "He doesn't even look like an athlete," Murphy grumbled.

What matter? What did looks count against the kind of soaring hope that wrapped the Mets in silk and French perfume, as separate from reality as a lover's dream?

Leonard Shecter

Hope flowed with such a rush that there was even talk about the Mets finishing fifth, or fourth, or third. The dreams were sweet in those days.

Of course the Mets had to take a look at Pappas. Because there was always that chance that the Devil had conspired to deliver Douglass *(The Year the Yankees Lost the Pennant)* Wallop's Shoeless Joe Hardy, and that the first time he threw a baseball smoke would rise from the mitt and the catcher's hand would come out of it looking like a bag of peanuts. You don't fool around with the Devil.

Murphy wouldn't let Pappas work out on the hallowed ground of the Mets' playing field. He took him down to some empty lot and all the people covering the club went along, eyes shining, pulses pounding. Then the skinny kid with all the hair started to warm up and it was all over. He was no Shoeless Joe. He was no Herb Score. He couldn't even throw very hard. Indeed, he couldn't throw at all.

Johnny Murphy shook his head sadly. "All you have is guts, son," he said.

"I would always have wondered," John Pappas said. "But now I know. I just wasn't good enough. Now I'll look for something else, some other way of being somebody."

And then he said, "I'm sorry they didn't give me a chance to hit. I'm not a bad hitter, you know. And I play the outfield, too."

There were many other false hopes raised that spring. Take Marshall Hamilt, a heavy-legged young man who had changed his first name to Dawes because he liked the way it sounded. ("Are you Jewish?" he said to everyone

Once Upon a Time . . .

he met. "I'm Jewish.") Hamilt had signed for a $3,700 bonus the previous August and by September he was in St. Petersburg working out. He had left a job with Sears, Roebuck in Boston that paid $1.65 an hour but had been unable to find one in St. Pete that paid more than $1.10. He was prepared to sacrifice and his enthusiasm was unbounded. But he was a terrible baseball player. Yet not much worse than another heavy-legged infielder named Bruce Fitzpatrick. These were the two rookies Casey Stengel chose to tout to the world as young pheenoms and future greats. He trotted them out for visiting columnists, and for one brief moment, Camelot. Then they had to play in real baseball games. They have never been heard of since.

"Everybody says 'I want to make the big league,' " a mildly irascible Stengel commented about this time. "If you can't make this club, with no regulars, what the hell are you?" Well, a John Pappas maybe, or a Dawes Hamilt, or a Bruce Fitzpatrick. There were those, alas, who weren't even good enough for that incredible first year of the Mets.

All sorts of people showed up in that Met camp. There was a pitcher named Butterball Botz, who was so bad Dawes Hamilt could hit line drives off him. One of them even managed to hit Botz. Hamilt ran halfway out to the mound to apologize.

Of course, once the Mets had established themselves in tenth place they protected their properties with a pitching screen. But in that first spring everybody had to show how brave he was.

Among those who drifted into camp was Clem Labine, a Brooklyn favorite. Weiss wanted as many ex-Dodgers

Leonard Shecter

and ex-Giants on his team as possible and would cheerfully have resurrected Mel Ott. Labine had been cut loose by the Pirates after a 4–1 relief season and nobody called him, except George Weiss. Labine said it would be lovely to be playing in New York again. Except he didn't make it. There were some things about the Mets that were genuinely sad, and that was one of them.

Stengel always had a great eye for talent and he soon fastened his left one, the one that glittered, on Al Jackson, the left-handed pitcher. This means he singled him out for special instructions and long-winded essays. "He rambles a little bit," Jackson said. "But I think I understand him."

Actually there was nothing to it. Stengel was asked what he had been telling Jackson and this is what he replied:

"I had a little chat with him because he's on the club. He's artistic. I know this because he was fielding the bunted balls. If he knew anything about himself I'd like him to tell me. What can you do pretty good? There might be two or three things that you don't know about yourself. He's an educated boy in many ways. He's alert like [Bobby] Shantz. And he's had 165 strikeouts, so he must know one or two things. If he's a pitcher and he's left-handed he might hold you to first base. I would like to know how you strike out 165. He's got a chance because how many pitchers have I got? He's very intelligent and his wife's a schoolteacher. I gave him a little quiz and he got it like that. [Stengel snapped his fingers.] I'm not gonna change your salary now but you can make some money with the Mets. You'll be in a big city and you can make outside money. And who found [Luis] Arroyo? To

Once Upon a Time . . .

tell you the truth the boy looks like a good fielder and he can sacrifice so you don't have to take him out and I heard he can play the outfield. I didn't say you're on the team, but you have a terrific chance. He looks like he's been pitching baseball for ten years. He has some flaws, but he looks very skillful."
Any questions?

Another in the zany cast of Met characters was Harold Apple. He was a twenty-four-year-old right-handed pitcher who had played basketball in the shadow of Jerry Lucas at Ohio State. He earned instant Met immortality because the first time he stepped onto the playing field at St. Petersburg he managed to get himself hit in the pitching arm by Iron Mike, the mechanical pitcher. He was the first casualty of the Met camp and was rushed to the hospital where x rays showed no serious injury.

Elio Chacon. The Mets had shelled out $75,000 to the Cincinnati Reds for him and sent him a contract in Caracas, Venezuela, where, rumor had it, Chacon lived and played winter baseball. No reply. They sent him a letter raising their salary offer. No answer. A cable. No answer. Two more cables. Silence.
Finally the Mets cabled Sherman Jones, another of their new properties, who was playing on the same team. The cable asked Jones to get Chacon to contact the Mets.
Jones told Chacon.
"He said O.K.," Jones was to recall. "That's all he ever said. That and yes and no, even when he talked Spanish."
In any case, the talk with Jones moved Chacon to send back his contract and ask for more money. The Mets came through, but again silence set in. Until, after the

training camp had opened, this cable was received: "I AM WAITING PASSAGE. ELIO."

Murphy wasn't sure what this meant, but he arranged with an airline to deliver a ticket to Chacon's door. Acknowledgment was not forthcoming for more than a week. Then this: "I WILL REACHED MONDAY. SICK PARENT. ELIO."

The airline told the Mets that Chacon was due at the Tampa airport at 10:57 of a Monday night and when the time came Lou Niss, the traveling secretary, a man who looked sad even when he was happy, was waiting. Chacon arrived 5 A.M. Tuesday. "I asked him what happened to his plane," Niss said. "I still haven't been able to figure out what he said." There was then a long press conference, the highlights of which went like this:

Q. During the World Series (between Cincinnati and the Yankees) you said you were going to get married. Did you?

A. I say only if we win the whole thing. (The Yankees won the Series.)

Q. What did you tell your girl friend?

A. I told her take it easy.

Q. Isn't she impatient?

A. No.

Q. Do you know what impatient means?

A. No.

It turned out he didn't know a lot about playing shortstop either, which is what the Mets needed him to do. Except the Mets were half a season finding out. They should have listened that spring to Jim Brosnan, the erudite Cincinnati pitcher. He was asked if Chacon could play shortstop. "Why should he?" Brosnan said. "He couldn't play second base."

The Mets always found things out too late.

Once Upon a Time . . .

One of George Weiss's dazzling cash pickups was Richie Ashburn. Of course, Ashburn was thirty-five years old at the time, had slowed up in the field, and his .300 lifetime batting average was represented by a mere .257 the year before with the Cubs. Yet there was still magic to the man, in the field, where he somehow managed to reach the ball most of the time; at the bat, where he could still hit record numbers of fouls while waiting for the pitcher to throw that fatal fourth ball; and in the clubhouse, where he was the first to plug into the Met mystique, the first to understand, hey, there's something funny about all this; we're standing at the edge of greatness and all we have to do is fall in. Push!

The first thing Ashburn said when he arrived in St. Petersburg was that he always wanted to play in New York—with the Yankees. But it was his old teammate Robin Roberts the Yankees picked up and Ashburn had to settle for the Mets. He tried to be philosophical about it. "I sort of like the Polo Grounds," he said. "I remember I hit three home runs there in one series, two off Johnny Antonelli and one off Ruben Gomez. I said to myself, 'Boy oh boy, this is my home-run year.' The rest of the season I hit one more."

Ashburn never hit more than four home runs in a season in his life. But the Mets didn't get him to hit home runs. They got him to play center field. Ashburn thought he'd be pretty good at it. "The Polo Grounds is narrow," he said. "You don't see many balls drop between fielders out there."

Not, at least, until the Mets arrived.

The day the regulars reported they made jokes. They looked at each other and understood that this was like a reunion of French Foreign Legionnaires. They knew that what they had left, by and large, was pride. It should never be forgotten, Virginia, that the Mets, even before that first terrible season started, had pride.

Jim Marshall, elderly first baseman, had been a holdout for a while and finally signed at a slight increase. He said it was awful coming south without a contract. "I was sitting next to a kid name of Bailey from the Braves," he said. "He got $170,000 to sign. It was terrible."

Gil Hodges. After an hour in the sun, Hodges was seen to be sweating heavily and limping a lot. "Not too bad for the first day," he said. He limped off into the clubhouse.

It was remarked that the balls were not flying out of Miller Huggins Field, where the Mets trained, the way they had when the Yankees trained there. Ted Lepcio, a man who had been described as the world's worst ballplayer, hit one out. At least Gil Hodges, who was in the outfield, told him he had. But Hodges had a reputation as a great kidder and Lepcio doubted the whole thing.

"I hit one out last Monday," said Chris Cannizzaro. "But the wind was blowing out a gale."

"I hit one out, too, the first day," Joe Ginsberg, the catcher, said to a reporter. "But don't put it in the paper. They'll expect too much of me. Write about the ball I hit over second base."

At the end of the workout Gus Bell said, "I think I'll go home and lay the body down for a while."

The pitchers in that first Met camp will always remember it. The pitching coach was Red Ruffing. He believed pitchers should run. "You can tell if they're out of shape," Ruffing always said. "They vomit. When they stop, they're in shape."

History should record the lineups of the Mets' first intrasquad game, which Casey Stengel called a yannigan. In the old days intrasquad games were always played between the Yannigans and Brannigans. On this day in the hot spring of 1962 they were called the Lavagettos and the Hemuses, after the coaches.

The Lavagettos	*The Hemuses*
Ashburn, cf	Drake, 2b
Zimmer, 3b	Fitzpatrick, ss
Bell, rf	Christopher, cf
Thomas, lf	Bouchee, 1b
Marshall, 1b	Chrisley, rf
Mantilla, ss	Hickman, lf
Lepcio, 2b	Hamilt, 3b
Landrith, c	Ginsberg, c
Craig, p	Anderson, p

Missing from the first team, or Lavagettos, were Gil Hodges, 1b, and Charley Neal, 2b. Old bones were wilting in the heat.

Baseball players love to talk about money when it's somebody else's. Most of them, particularly the old-timers, never publicly reveal their salaries. Often though, when it becomes ancient history, players are willing to reminisce about their old primitive wages. To illustrate that the original Met ballplayers were, if nothing else, typical, we have the story of Gus Bell. Bell was involved in what has become known as a classic bad trade. Certainly it had to be the worst Branch Rickey ever made.

Bell was sent by Rickey, then running the Pittsburgh club, to Cincinnati for what amounted to Cal Abrams. The Indians made a better deal when they sold Manhattan. That was ten years before the Mets came into existence, years which Bell spent happily hitting a total of 176 home runs and batting in 770 runs for the Reds. No one knows what happened to Abrams.

Rickey never made a trade like that by accident and Bell agreed. "We didn't get along," he said. "I think it started when he took over the club. I'd had what I felt were two pretty good seasons and the first thing I read he said about me was he wasn't sure if I was ready to play major league ball. I was twenty-three years old and sitting on the bench because he had a youth movement going and was playing Class C ballplayers."

But what it really came to was a salary dispute. For some strange reason, when it came to signing his 1952 contract, Bell thought he was worth more than Rickey thought.

"How much salary were you getting then?" Bell was asked.

"I'd rather not say," said Bell. "I never did say and I'm not going to say now."

Ballplayers change, but not very much.

It should be noted that the first Met ball game, their intrasquad game, started out in what was to become fine Met tradition. Sammy Drake, the first batter, was missing. So Joe Ginsberg went up to bat for him. With the count one and one, Drake came out of the clubhouse and took over. He hit a triple.

Once Upon a Time . . .

"See how smart Casey is?" Ginsberg said. "Puts a pinch hitter in for the leadoff hitter and he gets a triple. No wonder he won so many pennants."

It was a television commercial. The idea was that Casey Stengel, the marvelous manager of the amazing Mets, had gotten into an argument with an umpire which so upset him he needed a Bromo-Seltzer to calm his stomach. It was a time when the Federal Communications Commission was attempting to crack down on people who endorsed products they really didn't use. So one of the flunkies from the advertising agency said to Stengel, "You use Bromo-Seltzer, don't you?"

"Why sure," Stengel said. "Only I never get sick, so I don't have to."

At any rate the commercial was filmed and most of the trouble came from Stengel overacting his bellyache. "That's a little too much," the director said.

"You mean you don't want me to die?" Stengel said. "I'm old enough."

And for the next weeks, whenever Stengel referred to the filming of the commercial, he said he did it for Alka-Seltzer.

Roger Craig worked as hard, or harder, than anybody else in that first Met camp. He'd been a Dodger all his playing life and resented them for letting him go. His idea was to make them sorry they had. So the tall, thin Craig, with the receding chin that made him look like Slim Summerville, went to work. Even before he came to Florida, he was throwing baseballs in anger. In camp he was in better shape than any other pitcher, and as he worked and sweated it became obvious that he would be the

Leonard Shecter

pitcher who had the honor of starting the Mets' first exhibition game. Sure enough, he was picked. Carefully saving his arm the day before this historic event, Craig didn't do any throwing at all. Instead he ran in the outfield and then went over to the sliding pit. "Not that I'm on base so much," the conscientious Craig said. "It's just that I should practice in case I am and want to break up a double play."

He didn't break up any double plays. He broke up Roger Craig. He pulled a muscle in his pitching shoulder in the sliding pit and the man who started against St. Louis in the first exhibition game was Jay Hook.

Hook lost. He also pulled a muscle in his shoulder and was out ten days.

It has become a sort of tradition to believe that the Mets fooled everybody, including the reporters who covered them, that everybody thought that they were actually going to be good. That's only partly true. As evidence I submit portions of a dispatch I sent to the New York *Post* on the eve of the Mets' first exhibition game:

"What can be said about the Mets lineup? It's elderly, it's a little slow, the power is mostly a memory. Yet it's certainly a better lineup than the Houston club will be able to field and there are some who insist it's better than anything the Cubs and Phillies can muster.

"Let's take it from the top of Casey Stengel's batting order. Richie Ashburn, cf. Ashburn is thirty-five, a big man among the Young Republicans in Tilden, Nebraska, the father of six children, and a great fellow. He hit .257 with the Cubs last year, still has a good enough eye to draw a lot of walks. Of his 79 hits last season (he only had 307 at bats) seven were doubles, four triples. He hit his last home run in 1959. 'When I could still run,' he says, 'I could go get them with anybody including Willie Mays.' But he can't anymore and the Polo Grounds has a big center field.

"Don Zimmer, 3b. Zimmer is a funny little man and a noisy type infielder. He likes to play golf and the horses. He's thirty-one years old and last year hit .252 for the Cubs. He's a play-me-or-trade-me type and if he ever has to say that to Stengel the Mets will be in trouble for a third baseman.

"Charlie Neal, 2b. He seems like the best professional on the ball club. He's thirty-one years old, still looks efficient around second base although last year the Dodgers were saying he'd had it, both at bat and in the field. He hit .235 in 108 games in Los Angeles, blames his troubles on injuries and illness.

"Frank Thomas, lf. Club slugger. He's got to be Mickey Mantle and Roger Maris all rolled into one for the Mets. Thomas is thirty-two, the father of six and has the best hitting record of any Met. He batted .284 with the Braves, hit 25 home runs and had 67 RBI's. He's being counted on for more than he could ever deliver.

"Gus Bell, rf. Even Stengel has noticed that Bell has been having trouble hitting the ball in batting practice. He's thirty-three years old and hit .255 playing part-time with the Reds last season. Once a big homer hitter, he hit three last year. He's got seven children. (The Met outfield has 19 children altogether and those concerned have spent weeks down here trying to find some significance to it.)

"Gil Hodges, 1b. Each year, Hodges says, it's a little more difficult getting into shape. This year Hodges is pushing thirty-seven and he'll be in shape no matter how difficult it is. The wise boys are betting, though, that he can't play much more than half the Mets games, if that. Old bones can't take the abuse. But you'll never hear him complain.

"Felix Mantilla, ss. The Mets have been so impressed with the work of the twenty-seven-year-old Mantilla who hit .215 in 45 games with Milwaukee last year that they are frantically looking elsewhere for a shortstop. Elio Chacon will get a trial, but the Mets are liable to settle for a triple-A hitter with a good glove. That is, if they can find one.

"Hobie Landrith, c. Good catchers are hard to find and Landrith is one. He handles young pitchers well and at thirty-one is far from used up. But the Giants, who have Willie Mays and Orlando Cepeda, didn't think they could afford his bat. He hit .239 in 43 games last year. His best year was 1959, when he hit .251 in 109 games. The Mets will be content if he does as well for them.

"The pitching is another story. It may be just as grim. Whatever the story is, though, it will show up during the exhibition season. Until now Stengel could get away just talking. Now they're going to put the scores in the paper."

The Mets lost their first exhibition game to the St. Louis Cardinals, 8–0, and people throughout the civilized world were struck by the same joke: It's not a matter of whether the Mets will ever win a game, it's just a matter of whether they will score a run.

The next day it looked like the answer was that they never would. Hearts quickened when Chris Cannizzaro hit a long fly ball in the third. The crowd, 2,574 strong, all elderly, all Met fans, cheered when Frank Thomas hit one over the left field fence and into Tampa Bay in the

Once Upon a Time...

fourth. But the ball, alas, curved foul, and only those who had been there knew this was a home run in the Polo Grounds. Immediately "Home run in the Polo Grounds" became a Met rallying cry, like "Geronimo" or "Remember the Alamo."

The jokes began.

"What's going to happen to these guys in July, when they get tired?"

"When do we get the three Card pitchers together and ask them when they first knew they had the no-hitter?"

The man who broke the schneid was Choo Choo Coleman, and it was a move by Stengel, the thinking man's manager, which set history in motion. Coleman was a pinch hitter. Stengel never thought better, even when he was with the Yankees.

Coleman's eighth-inning home run over the hard-to-reach right-field fence in Al Lang Field was a two-run job, and the Mets soon had another run and a tie score. In the ninth Ed Bauta gave up a double to Richie Ashburn. Then Elio Chacon knocked him in with the winner. The score was 4–3. And the date was March 12, 1962.

Well before the season started, last place had been unanimously ceded to Houston. The Chicago Cubs, training out of sight and almost out of mind in Arizona, had been relegated to ninth. So the great battle for seventh place was to be between the Philadelphia Phillies and the Mets.

Gene Mauch, manager of the Phillies, was having none of it. "Look, I don't want to knock these guys," he said. But he did, he did.

He pointed out, for example, that while it was true enough that the Cubs had finished 17 games ahead of the

Phillies the year before, this was largely due to his club's freakish 23-game losing streak. Besides, he said, the Cubs on the Mets were not exactly the Cubs who had beaten the Phillies. "They beat us with Billy Williams and Ernie Banks and pitchers like Don Cardwell."

But Mauch knew what it was like to be a loser and he tried to soften his knock. "Maybe they're better than I think they are," he said. "But they're not going to do it down here, or with talk."

To prove it, he sent out his best warriors to destroy the Mets with one blow. They succeeded, but only barely, for the score was 3–2 and the Mets had runners at second and third when the mighty Choo Choo Coleman, he who smote the first Met home run, popped up to the shortstop for the final out. It was, no doubt, a portent.

Still, the big game of the spring was yet to come. It was the first titanic struggle between the new blood rivals of baseball, the Mets and the Yankees. Prestige was at stake, plus a bit of bad blood left over from when George Weiss left the Yankees with the understanding that he would take no job as general manager, only to show up as president of the Mets, a bit of pettifoggery that went down like a rising gorge. Weiss returned the anger of the Yankees with ill-feigned disdain. In fact, he felt he had been forcibly retired while still at the peak of his power. Besides, the Yankees had fired Casey Stengel and the old man was not about to let them feel comfortable about it.

The battle would be fought on several grounds. Word had filtered up from Fort Lauderdale that the Yankees, when the Mets came down there, were going to entertain the press lavishly, that the usual bologna and sliced ham in the press room would give way to steak, chicken, and barbecued spareribs. The press was agog.

The Mets were willing to counter with caviar at forty

Once Upon a Time . . .

paces, but there was still the field of honor. For that you needed a ball club. This meant the Mets were in trouble.

In preparing for the great day, the Mets came off a seven-game losing streak to destroy the Detroit Tigers by a score of 1–0. The winning run was scored because Gus Bell hit a pinch triple (a providential move by the genius Stengel, since the wind was blowing in all day except for the precise moment Bell hit the ball) and Elio Chacon followed with a bunt. The Tigers were caught flat-footed.

As for the shutout, it was fashioned by Ray Daviault, Herb Moford and Bob Moorhead. Their names, too, decorate the honor roll of the Mets.

The first miracle of the Mets came on March 23, 1962. That's when they beat the Yankees, 4–3 in the bottom of the ninth after blowing a 3–2 lead in the top half. The winning run scored on a triple by Joe Christopher and a pinch single by Richie Ashburn. The Yankees were trying. Their pitchers were Bill Stafford and Ralph Terry, but Roger Craig pitched six innings for the Mets and held the Yankees to two runs.

After the game Casey Stengel walked into the special press room the Mets had set up. He was wearing a blue-serge suit, slicked-back hair, and a cat-that-ate-the-canary expression.

Those hard-nosed reporters, radio and TV men present, who had geen guzzling Mrs. C. S. Payson's booze and gobbling her caviar and hors d'oeuvres, broke into applause.

Stengel raised his large hands and waved them like a Philharmonic conductor deprecating applause and asking for silence. "It shows you," he said, "how easy this business is."

Stengel never kidded himself, however. Amid all the

optimistic enthusiasm that surrounded the Mets, Stengel remained an island of sanity. Oh, he staged his little charades, trotting out Dawes Hamilt and Bruce Fitzpatrick before visiting columnists, but Stengel always knew where he was. Like after his first great victory someone said to the old man, "How much do you like Christopher?"

"Love him, love him," Stengel said in his best falsetto. "Tonight I love him. Yesterday I didn't. Anyway, I think he's got a bad back."

Stengel also said, "I'm glad we did good. It's good for the club. But we ain't so great. My pitcher didn't throw the ball over to first base so they got down and broke up two double plays. It was a good game, but we still did the same thing with men on base [not hit]. I don't know when they're going to learn."

Once Stengel got this one off:

"Most of our hitters are what? Putsie-downsies." He took a weak half swing, half bunt, to illustrate.

Another time, a fan horned in on a Stengel press conference to say: "That Zimmer's the guts of your club, isn't he?"

Well, Zimmer was doing all right. He was one of those people it's supposed to be good to have around your club because he always tries so hard. In fact, though, his range around third base had become limited and his hitting soon proved illusory. Stengel must have known it all the time, for what he said to the fan was: "Why, he's beyond that. He's much more. He's the perdotious quotient of the qualificatilus. He's the lower intestine."

Rod Kanehl. At twenty-eight, Kanehl had been in baseball eight years without playing in a major-league ball game. Casey Stengel remembered him from a spring

Once Upon a Time . . .

he'd spent with the Yankees, particularly a day in which a ball was hit over Kanehl's head and the outfield fence. Running after the ball, Kanehl went right on up and over the fence, picked it up and climbed back on to the field. Stengel was indelibly impressed and when he saw Kanehl's name on a list of availables, he pointed a gnarled old finger and said: "I want him."

This was one of the areas in which Stengel and George Weiss were to have a running battle. One time Stengel reported a conversation he had with Weiss about Kanehl. "Weiss says, 'I ain't seen him do anything in the field,' " Stengel rasped. "So I said, 'You're full of baloney, he can run the bases.' "

And not a great deal more, although before long he was to play every position for the Mets except pitcher and catcher, all of them with aplomb, none of them especially well. Right from the beginning, though, things happened to Kanehl that you put into threatening letters. At his first opportunity he pulled a muscle so badly that his leg took on the color of a tropical sunset and he couldn't walk for a week. The first time he got into a game—as a late-inning sub—the first ball hit to him went through his legs and he pulled another muscle.

The next time he played—second base—he threw two double-play balls into the dirt, and when he was tried at third he was fooled on two pop fouls that dropped with sickening little thuds onto the ground behind him. (In fact, Kanehl never did learn to play second base, which he played a lot. What he couldn't do was make that flying double-play pivot. So he would plant himself on the bag and take the sliding runner's spikes in the shins. He made the DP, but he played three years with bleeding shins.)

It wasn't until late March, that first spring, that Rod

Leonard Shecter

Kanehl became a Met. It was against Sandy Koufax and the Dodgers. With runners on second and third in the ninth and the Mets down 3–1, Kanehl was called on to pinch-hit. This was a revolting development since Kanehl was sleeping off a terrible hangover in a corner of the dugout. When he walked out into the sun he decided that as punishment he had been struck blind.

Kanehl let the first pitch go by. "It was a good pitch," he was to say afterward, a crooked smile on his face, his dark eyes glinting with amusement. "A hummer. With hair on it. I mean it sounded like a good pitch. I didn't see it."

The next pitch was a curve ball and it fooled Kanehl completely. He thought it was going to be a high fast ball, started to swing, realized it was a curve as it headed down at him and ducked away to save his life. The ball hit his bat anyway and after that it just naturally took itself down along the first-base line and Kanehl had a base hit. Two runs scored. Shocked, Koufax gave up a hit to Felix Mantilla, and the Mets won 4–3. That's how Rod Kanehl became a Met hero. Indeed, the very first Met banner hung in the Polo Grounds read:

WE LOVE THE METS
ROD KANEHL

When the time came that Kanehl no longer got so many lucky hits, this man who somehow represented the spirit of the team—a spirit of cheerful, willing, spirited, hilarious failure—was cut off without a backward glance. Worse, when the Yankees wanted to give him a job as minor-league manager, Weiss demanded a player in payment. The Yanks refused and Kanehl went home. No-

Once Upon a Time . . .

body on the Mets even thought to give him a job as coach. Yogi Berra got a job as coach. When you come right down to it, what the hell does Yogi Berra have to do with the Mets?

The snares and the delusions of the Mets could sometimes be pinpointed in one place, in one man. Charley Neal. In 1959 at the age of twenty-eight Neal was the heart of the Dodger infield, playing both second base and shortstop, making the memorable play everyplace including the World Series, and hitting .287 while knocking in 83 runs. In the next two seasons he crumbled, simply fell apart. Instead of making the big play, he made the big error. When it was time for the big hit, he hit into a double play. It was said around the Dodgers that Neal couldn't play the game anymore. It started, they said, when he began to hot-dog it, making the easy plays look hard. In time the easy plays became hard and he lost his confidence.

No matter how it happened, Neal promptly showed all his strengths and weaknesses with the Mets. At first there were gasps of surprise that a Met, even one that cost $275,000, should be able to execute plays with such precision. At one point Stengel was moved to remark, "If you watch all the second basemen in the country, you'd have to say that Neal can do what any of them can. He looks like he's worth what we paid for him."

In a short time, though, Neal was making the kind of play that induced the Dodgers to dump him. All illusions that the Dodgers had given him up because they were basically sympathetic to the New York cause disappeared. Charley Neal, it was obvious, had become a losing ballplayer; in short, a Met.

Leonard Shecter

On March 26, Jay Hook, mechanical engineer, pitcher, was kept in an exhibition ball game in Miami against Baltimore until he had given up 17 hits. The Mets lost 18–8, which wasn't so bad. It was far from customary, however, to allow a young pitcher to take that kind of beating, and one can only put it down to one of Stengel's flashes of irascibility. Later, Hook was to go on to win the Mets' first league game, to stop their first long losing streak, and to become the first Met pitcher to beat the Dodgers in New York. But on that March 26 he was upset enough to cry.

The situation reminded Richie Ashburn of a story. "It was in the minor leagues," he said. "I saw a team bat around three times on Warren Hacker. Now the manager goes to take him out and he's mad. 'You can't take me out now,' Hacker says. 'I know I can get this guy out. I've got him out twice this inning.' "

Butterball Botz. One of the things expansion did was turn baseball into a field of newly plowed hope, warm and loamy. Butterball Botz was being ignored on the Mets. The press was concentrating on such famous characters as Choo Choo Coleman, Aubrey Gatewood, and Howie Nunn. Botz, bought conditionally from the Milwaukee Braves (conditionally meant the Mets could return him if they wished and get most of their money back, the kind of deal which George Weiss seems to have invented) was hidden in the shadows of these giants. But slowly he compiled a record of six runless innings, which sent a lot of people, including Casey Stengel, to the record book, where Butterball was revealed to have had a 2.11 earned run average in Triple-A the season before.

Botz had been in the minor leagues for six years and

Once Upon a Time . . .

it was wondered how the big brains of baseball could have been so mistaken about him. Big brains can make big mistakes, Botz pointed out. "Didn't Lou Burdette get away from the Yankees?" he would ask.

Botz learned control with Milwaukee watching Burdette and Warren Spahn fool the hitters each spring and decided he could make it even if he didn't have the kind of arm that could throw BB's. And things were, in the immortal words of Casey Stengel, going splendid, until one day in Pompano Beach when Butterball pitched against the Washington Senators. Botz came on in the fifth inning and gave up five quick runs. Two of them scored on a home run hit over the high fence in dead center by Dale Long. The home run prompted a press box wit to remark that Butterball would now be known as Longball. After that it was all downhill. When last heard of Botz was selling plastic bowling balls.

When the Mets played the Yankees again, this time in Fort Lauderdale, it turned out that the Yankees' secret weapon wasn't steak and spareribs at all. It was a chicken. She was about eighteen years old and dressed in Polynesian costume—grass skirt and bare bellybutton. She served daiquiries and other varied potions along with some tasty island tidbits in the press box, presumably so that nobody would notice that on the field the Mets were again beating the Yankees.

In the fifth the Mets were ahead, by 2–1 and one old-line Yankee type was moved to remark: "Shows you why baseball is giving way to football. Take a bunch of culls and bums, give them a pitcher, and they stand off the world champions."

The pitcher was Roger Craig and in the seventh inning

he got into trouble. With the score 2–2 the bases were loaded and Mickey Mantle was coming to the plate. The Yankeephiles (you could tell which they were, they weren't looking at the girl) were gloating in anticipation. On the field, Casey Stengel, self-confessed slickest manager in baseball, went out to the mound for a talk with Craig.

After Stengel left, Mantle swung on the first pitch, sent a two-hopper to Gil Hodges at first base and Craig was out of the inning.

"Stengel," said a wit, "told Mantle to hit the ball to Hodges on two hops."

What Stengel actually said was, "You got no bases open. What are you going to do with him?"

"Get him out," Craig said.

That's what he did, too, and things looked grim for the Yankees. But in the eighth the old Yankee luck asserted itself. With Al Jackson pitching and one on Elston Howard hit a double-play ball to Felix Mantilla at shortstop. At the last moment the ball hopped over the shortstop's head. So the Yankees won the game 3–2 on Moose Skowron's sacrifice fly.

"I wanted to win it," said Ralph Houk, the Yankee manager. "I didn't want you sons of bitches putting us on the front page again."

There were losers even among the losers. Ted Lepcio. In 1961 Lepcio played for three teams. He hit .183 with Syracuse, and a total of .167 with Chicago and Minnesota in the big league. This kind of thing is not calculated to make a manager sit up and take notice. Still, it was the Mets who went after Lepcio and not vice versa.

So by the end of March Lepcio wanted to know how

Once Upon a Time . . .

come spring training was almost finished and he'd played only a total of two innings?

Why didn't he ask Stengel?

"The hell with that," Lepcio said. "He knows I'm here. I'm not going to go begging him to play me."

At thirty-one, Lepcio was well acquainted with the methods of drawing attention to yourself. One of them was to pop off to reporters. And that's what he had been doing. "But I haven't been able to get anybody to stand still and listen to me," he said. "Nobody even talks to me, not even the coaches. It's like I had the plague or something."

Obviously the Mets had Lepcio in case they needed a utility infielder. But the Mets had too many infielders. They had Charley Neal and Elio Chacon and Felix Mantilla and Don Zimmer and the apple of Stengel's eye, Rod Kanehl. Besides, the Minnesota Twins had just released Billy Martin and Stengel was after Weiss to bring him aboard. Weiss refused. But that didn't do poor Lepcio any good.

Still, by now he must be remembering that terrible spring with fondness. It isn't everybody who was once almost a Met.

By the end of that first spring Roger Craig had pitched 35 innings of exhibition baseball and had a 2.50 ERA. He was the Bob Feller of the Mets, the real perdotious quotient of the qualificatilus. Let's see, if Craig wins 25 games . . .

But there were carpers. Al Lopez, manager of the Chicago White Sox, for example. "A guy throwing breaking stuff is most effective in the spring," Lopez said after Craig had looked great against the Sox. "Craig's got good

53

control, and a good slider, and they're effective now because you don't see that many breaking balls."

Translation: Let's see how he does on the big diamonds.

There was another knock from an unexpected source. Johnny Keane, the kindly little manager of the St. Louis Cardinals, had watched the Mets hold his sluggers to one run in 17 innings. So it was suggested that he might be interested in a trade, maybe, huh, please? Like give up a lot for a little?

Keane said no thank you. "I don't think they have anything we'd be interested in. Roadblock Jones would have to be a starter and he's not as good as the ones we have now."

But how about this marvelous little lefthander, Al Jackson?

"That's what I was saying," Keane said. "He pitches a hell of a game. Keeps the hitters off stride. But you wonder about it. You try to picture him winning in the major leagues and you wonder."

Lopez and Keane were not exactly wrong about Craig and Jackson. But they were not exactly right either. It's one of the reasons that in the era of Joe Namath people still go to baseball games.

The Mets wound up with a 13–15 spring record, Zimmer hit .400, Kanehl, hitting baseballs that had eyes, wound up at .440, and George Weiss wound up sore. He was sore because he wanted the Mets to finish at .500 and it would have been closer if a losing game against the Dodger B team hadn't been included in the record.

"Would you have counted it if we won?" Weiss kept asking. He was told it was none of his business. He took

Once Upon a Time . . .

this with fairly good grace, because he was trying. Before he left Florida he actually sent word up to the press box in St. Pete asking if anybody had any questions. To the men who knew him when he was general manager of the Yankees, this was like a Burchite inviting a Pravda man to breakfast. "I want to thank you fellows," Weiss told reporters. "You've been very kind."

A year before, Weiss thought all newspaper men must have their kind glands removed as a condition of employment. But he was changing a lot. He even agreed to have his picture taken with Miss Rheingold and a beagle.

It was a scene out of Alice in Wonderland, the tea party perhaps; mad conversation, with Casey Stengel playing all the parts.

It started because an intrepid reporter (National League type) asked Stengel for his opening-day lineup. It was not altogether an unreasonable request since the Mets opening game was less than thirty hours away and the public was panting. But it was counting without Stengel's private world, the one in which he stored lineup cards, acres of them, shuffling them lovingly behind drawn window shades.

Give the old man this. He tried. In Yankee days he would have snapped out a "Why the hell should I tell you my lineup when the game ain't until tomorrow?" But the Mets were public-relations conscious. So Stengel tried. He really did.

He was dressing in front of his locker in the little echoing office at the Polo Grounds where once the golden tones of Leo Durocher reverberated. He concentrated so hard he had left off only one item of apparel when he finished dressing—his pants.

"Neal," Stengel boomed finally, and it was as though it had been torn out of him. "He's first. Then Chacon."

"Chacon?" a reporter said.

"Mantilla," Stengel answered, pronouncing the Ls hard, so that the name came out harsh instead of musical. "I mean Chacon. I mean I said Chacon but I meant Mantilla."

He paused and rummaged in his locker, finally went off looking for his shoes. "I don't know who to hit third," he said. "If it's a right-handed pitcher, which it is, I might go with Bell in right field."

Suddenly he turned angry. "You asked me for a lineup and I can't give it to you," he snapped.

It was like asking a miser for a sample of his money. The clutch of reporters sat hushed, as though they were at a wake. They were starting to feel sorry for the old man. It was tearing him up.

"I got two centerfielders," he grumbled. "Christopher and Smith."

The reporters looked blank. Stengel had just gotten through telling them he was sending Joe Christopher to Syracuse.

"Christopher?" a reporter said.

"Ashburn," Stengel answered. "Smith and Ashburn. Whichever one I play I'll put leading off."

This was somewhat puzzling. As far as anybody could tell Stengel had said that Charley Neal would lead off and play second base, Felix Mantilla would bat second and play shortstop, Gus Bell bat third and play right field. Now he had Richie Ashburn or Bobby Gene Smith leading off.

Once Upon a Time...

"Didn't you say Neal was going to lead off?" Stengel was asked.

"Well," Stengel said annoyed, "put Neal third and Mantilla second." He stared into the locker as he pulled on his socks, mumbling to himself. "Let's see. You can put Hodges fifth. No, put Bell fifth. [See, he had to move Bell because he'd moved Neal.] Hodges sixth."

Stengel padded over to where a reporter was sitting and peered over his shoulder into his notebook. "Better write it down," he said, "so I'll remember it. And put Marshall along with Hodges. Maybe I'll put Hodges in for a while and then Marshall."

"Who you got hitting fourth?" Stengel was asked.

He looked puzzled. "Thomas," another reporter answered for him. "That right Case? Thomas in left field batting fourth?"

"That's right," Stengel said, and sighed as though he were through. But there were two positions remaining. Was it Don Zimmer at third and batting seventh? Stengel looked puzzled. He nodded vaguely.

"One more thing," a reporter said. "Who's the catcher, Landrith or Ginsberg?"

"It's Ginsberg or Landrith," Stengel said positively. "Ginsberg caught him [Roger Craig] pretty good. I'll decide when I get there."

This was the process by which Casey Stengel made up his lineup every day. But usually, it all happened inside his head.

This then was Casey Stengel's first genuine complete New York Mets lineup. It was made out on the night of April 11th in St. Louis, Missouri, in the year of our Lord 1962.

Leonard Shecter

        Ashburn, cf
        Mantilla, ss
        Neal, 2b
        Thomas, lf
        Bell, rf
        Hodges, 1b
        Zimmer, 3b
        Landrith, c
        Craig, p

    The day before the Mets were to play their first National League game, the lads were waiting for an elevator in the lobby of the Hotel Chase, in St. Louis, all dressed in their new team blazers which could only be described as Dodger blue. The elevator came. It was soon full. The boys in the back pushed. More got in. Altogether, there were sixteen Mets in the elevator when it jammed between floors. They were stuck for twenty minutes. "I knew it," Craig said in the elevator. "The first time in my life I'm going to open a season, I get stuck in an elevator. I'll probably be here for twenty-four hours."

    "It wasn't so bad for the other guys," Hobie Landrith, the short catcher, said. "I'm not built high enough. I couldn't get any air down where I was."

    The Mets were rained out of their first game. They opened the next night, and their first hit was a single up the middle by Gus Bell in the second, and then Don Zimmer got the first Met hit with a man on base. To Landrith went the distinction of being the first Met hitter to pop up with two on and two out thus leaving the first Mets on base. It was a record to be tied by many.

    In the third inning Hobie Landrith made a bad throw

Once Upon a Time...

(on a pitchout yet) and Curt Food had a stolen base. It did not seem important at the time, but it was unquestionably precedent setting.

It was altogether fitting and proper that the Mets' first home run should be hit by Gil Hodges. He did it in the fourth. It can also be recorded that the first hit by a Met in a lost cause was a double by Mantilla in the seventh by which time the Mets were down 10–4. The game was lost 11–4 and a reporter suggested to Casey Stengel that all he could do now was pray things got better. Said Stengel: "I don't know about that. Prayers don't win for you. You got to do it yourself."

After the game Don Zimmer said he couldn't understand it. "We're big enough," he said, "our uniforms fit. Hell, we look like the Yankees."

It was good on Opening Day in New York to see the Polo Grounds come alive again, brash bunting billowing in the damp breeze, fresh paint brightening the gloomy day. The Polo Grounds, long empty, was an old friend, so long unvisited you'd almost forgotten its once familiar, comfortable old face. Nostalgia dripped like an ice-cream cone in the sun. The pull hitters like Frank Thomas remembered the home runs they had hit there and the short hitters like Solly Hemus and Richie Ashburn remembered they liked to play there because the fences were in reach. For others it was the chunks of history, the ghosts hovering in the outfield and echoing in the dugouts.

It was a ball park of an old and vanishing school, the Polo Grounds, wood rather than concrete, a fortune wasted in obstructed views, yet there was an unmatched intimacy with the game on the field for all of that. Ebbets

Leonard Shecter

Field in Brooklyn had it and Griffith Stadium in Washington and the St. Louis ball park before it was torn down. The Polo Grounds was a lovable freak. Its oval shape made it a polo grounds indeed, even if it was not conceived as such. So it was only 257 feet down the right field line (they'll tell you Johnny Mize could spit that far) and 279 feet down the left, and centerfield was so far away only one man, Joe Adcock, had ever hit a ball into the seats out there. As a result, freak things had happened at the Polo Grounds. The players, coming back to a place they performed in when much younger, remembered them with great warmth.

Gil Hodges, of course, recalled the Bobby Thomson home run which gave the Giants their miracle pennant in 1951. "I suppose he hit it pretty good," Hodges said, "but it was a low line drive and it just got in. It didn't make it by much."

"Would it have been a home run in any other park in the league?"

"No," Hodges said. Then he said it louder, "No!"

Ralph Branca, who was the pitcher that ill-starred day, was on hand for the Polo Grounds opener, too. He stood on the steps of the visitors' dugout, wearing a topcoat and a still sad look on his face, and pointed toward left field. "He didn't hit it real good," Branca said. "It was a sinking line drive with a lot of down spin on it. Any place else it's an easy out. It just dropped in there between 33 and 34."

There was no way to see the section numbers on the girders from where Branca was standing, but he knew the numbers by heart and presumably he always will. One section past the foul pole, a game, a pennant, maybe a career looped into the seats between 33 and 34.

Dick Groat, who broke in at the Polo Grounds and

Once Upon a Time...

had some of his good days there, remembered the place fondly. The Pirate shortstop recalled a day in 1952 when the Pirates were leading the Giants by a run in the sixth inning. "It started to rain and we were stalling," Groat said. "Dusty Rhodes was hitting and there was a man on base. He just barely ticked the ball, it hit the foul pole in right field and we were beat. By the time he got around the bases it was raining so hard you couldn't see him."

They were called Chinese home runs then. There were a lot of them hit and everybody had his own pet story. Gus Bell remembered how he broke up Sal Maglie's consecutive no-run inning streak on a pitch he misjudged.

"I was looking for a fast ball," Bell said, "and started to lean in on it. Only it was a slider. I pulled back, but I ticked the ball. It hit the screen on the foul pole about this much over the fence." He held his fingers three inches apart and looked embarrassed.

Don Hoak was with the Dodgers in 1954 and a home run that stuck with him was hit by Bobby Hofman of the Giants. "It was good and high and I remember there were three of us waiting for it to come down, the left fielder, Pee Wee Reese, and I. It was the tenth inning. We stood there under it, and at the last second the ball just scraped the scoreboard on the way down and we were beat."

Hoak sighed. "But I like the park," he said. "It's a nice old place."

It was at that.

The charm of the Polo Grounds, as it was for all the old, angular, billboard-decorated baseball parks, was that its shape was a factor in baseball games. Given a one-run lead in the late innings a pitcher had to try to avoid letting anybody pop the ball down the lines. Balls hit off the

Leonard Shecter

fence took funny bounces and only skilled outfielders played them well. There was mounting excitement as a fielder tried to dig a ball out of an awkward corner as runners raced around the bases. Those who saw Willie Mays run out from under his hat chasing a ball hit over his head in centerfield will never forget the sight. It had been five years since a baseball was hit in anger at the Polo Grounds when the Mets got there. It was old and crumbling. Yet there was a style to the old place, and a feeling. This feeling was a mixture of joy and despair, just the ingredients that made up the new team that had come to give the Polo Grounds its brief respite from inevitable doom. From the very first day the Mets got there till they left it forever after two seasons, that was the emotional mixture at the Polo Grounds, joy and despair.

Nothing went right that first day. Casey Stengel slammed the door of his newly built office, and when he tried to get back into it there was no key that fitted the lock. Workmen had to be summoned to disassemble the doorframe. Brian Sullivan of the Metropolitan Opera and the St. Camillus Band rendered "The Star-Spangled Banner." But not together. And when the lineup was announced on the PA, it had Gil Hodges' name in it, although he had begged off because of a painful knee. The field was sloshy and the day drippy and only some 12,000 people showed up to see the historic debut of the Mets. Yet there was a flavor to the day, a delicious zaniness that had left New York with the Giants and Dodgers.

With the zaniness, once more, National League baseball; graceful, as when Roberto Clemente of the Pirates, oozing talent from every pore, came to a full gallop in the muddy outfield in the third inning and made a gooey,

Mrs. Charles Shipman Payson adds Casey Stengel's autographed book to her other memorabilia, rumored to include $200,000,000.

United Press International Photo

Rod Kanehl, Charlie Neal and Chris Cannizzaro in ticker-tape parade up Broadway, 1962. The Mets hadn't yet fired a baseball in anger. They got the parade just for *living*.

Sports Illustrated Photo by Herb Scharfman

Richie Ashburn, left, and Gus Bell do what comes naturally in Met outfield.

Sports Illustrated Photo by Herb Scharfman

The ball Richie Ashburn isn't catching was the only one ever hit into that section of the Polo Grounds bleachers. Lou Brock of the St. Louis Cardinals hit it. The stairway at the left leads to the little balcony where the Mets played Juliet to their Romeo fans.

Wide World Photos

Who's on third? Both Frank Thomas (25) and Charlie Neal, one over quota. In the confusion, Phillies catcher Sammy White tagged the wrong man — Thomas — and Neal got back safely to second. It was one of Mets' finest hours. Unbelievers are Umpire Dusty Boggers and Ruben Amaro and Don Demeter (24) of Phillies.

Wide World Photos

Now Felix Mantilla has it, now he doesn't. Ball popped out of his glove but (gasp!) into glove of catcher Sammy Taylor.

Wide World Photos

One of the reasons Casey Stengel loved Rod Kanehl is that he would slide head first into first base. Bill White of the Cards seems surprised.

United Press International Photo

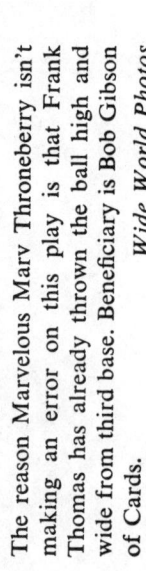

The reason Marvelous Marv Throneberry isn't making an error on this play is that Frank Thomas has already thrown the ball high and wide from third base. Beneficiary is Bob Gibson of Cards.

Wide World Photos

Casey Stengel's friend is Umpire Stan Landis.
United Press International Photo

Team photo was taken in 1963. Mets couldn't seem to find the birdie. Marvelous Marv Throneberry, top left, is looking for it in a special place, of course.

United Press International Photo

Once Upon a Time . . .

sliding catch of a foul ball hit by Richie Ashburn; and surprising, as when Dick Stuart, who came to be called Dr. Strangeglove, came up with a glorious diving catch of a line drive hit by Gus Bell in the fourth.

On the Mets' side Charley Neal made a marvelous play on a grounder by Smokey Burgess in the second and then in the sixth Frank Thomas earned 10,000 Green Stamps (when the Giants left, a home run was only worth a case of Wheaties) with a long home run into the upper deck in left field.

Of course the game turned on the kinds of play so many Met games were to turn on: a dropped ball (one that Bell and Ashburn let drop between them)', Marshall inexplicably coming off first base to take Neal's throw after the good play, two runs scoring with the help of wild pitches thrown by Herb Moford and Ray Daviault.

There was also the first delicious indication that these were not ordinary baseball fans, but Met fans, a new breed, many of them too young to remember the Giants and Dodgers, but wise and instinctively knowledgeable nevertheless. This was no Opening Day collection of bankers on a day off who didn't know or care about the game. This crowd made noise on every pitch, cheered called balls when the Mets were up, booed strikes.

Ashburn got a standing ovation for batting in the first Mets run with a single in the fifth. After Thomas's home run it sounded like 50,000 were cheering. But Bell was booed for letting the ball drop and Jim Marshall for coming off the bag, and the boys upstairs got on Daviault for being wild. Still, when Daviault struck out Dick Groat with the bases loaded in the ninth they turned around and cheered him. The Mets lost, 4–3, but the people had come to root for losers and they had a marvelous time doing it.

Leonard Shecter

There are some people now who insist that the first faint budding of "let's go Mets" was discovered that day. It was also discovered after the game that Casey Stengel's undershorts were still emblazoned with the emblem of the New York Yankees.

The Mets lost their first nine games. There was no way of throwing stones at individual players. You needed a blanket rather than a stone to get proper coverage. They all gave until it hurt. There was this game they lost to the Philadelphia Phillies, 11–9, for example. They lost it because Charley Neal let two routine balls get by him at second base. They lost it because Landrith was guilty of two passed balls. They lost it because Frank (Big Donkey) Thomas dropped an easy fly ball in left field. They lost it because of this kind of play:

In the second inning they were only three runs down. There were Phillies on first and third because Neal had let a line drive bounce off his glove. Tony Gonzales then hit a chopper back to the right side of the mound. Jim Marshall, the first baseman, came over for it. Craig Anderson, the pitcher, went after it and got it. He turned to throw it to first. Of course, no one was there. On the next play Zimmer couldn't find the handle on a little grounder and the Phillies had a five-run lead.

Stengel blamed Marshall. "Why should he go over there?" he grumbled. "He was out of place. No one knew where the hell he was."

Said Marshall: "Well, I don't know. I'm supposed to go for the ball until the pitcher calls me off. By the time he said anything, I was too far from the base to go back."

Then there was Neal. On a play like that, the second baseman ought to come over and cover first. Neal just

Once Upon a Time . . .

sort of stood there watching the play. And that was the Mets.

During the first losing streak Casey Stengel tried almost everything, including calling off a game because he alone detected a single raindrop. "To tell you the truth," he said, telling the truth, "I got two men crippled [Neal and Hodges] and if I'm winning I'll play five games a day for you. When you're losing, you don't bolster it that quick."

What made it even more humiliating was that he called off the game against Houston, the other expansion team, which at the time had a 3–2 record. By the time the Houstons left town, things were even more revolting. A couple of days later Stengel was forced even to be patient with a young reporter who suggested he play Gus Bell in centerfield in order to get Ed Bouchee into the lineup. The old man looked shocked, but he said gently, "I don't think you can do that. I don't think he can cover enough ground."

As Stengel was to say many times in the next years, there he was, the slickest manager in baseball, and he was getting the vaseline pot.

With the losing streak in full flower, Stengel called a workout at the Polo Grounds. "Can't lose today," grumbled Roger Craig, as he put on his uniform. "Dammit, we ought to have a victory party."

Stengel was of similar mind as he basked in the unaccustomed sunshine. "Can't lose today," he half sang, "lovely day, lovely day."

Soon, however, it was raining, and he was watching Don Zimmer in the batting cage. "Swinging too hard," Stengel said. Then, watching Jim Marshall, "See, he turns his head. If he don't turn his head he hits a line drive. Skowron is the only one I know turns his head and hits the ball anyway."

Stengel was always aware of what was the matter with the Mets, individually and all together.

The Mets were like every other team. After a loss the players stared into their lockers, drinking beer. After their ninth in a row on April 22nd, 1962, the locker starers were Sherman Jones, Don Zimmer, and Roger Craig. Each had earned a handsome share of the defeat Jones was charged with. But the ironies were beginning to get to the troops.

What got Craig, who was rated as the ace of what the Mets called their pitching staff, is that he'd had what he would call a good day. "This is one of the few times, maybe the only time," he said, "when they hit my good pitches, the ones I wanted to throw, and hit them well."

For a pitcher, this is a sort of end of the world. It's like a tightrope walker losing his nerve. When they hit your best pitches, thrown with control, you're either hexed or finished.

The Mets had nursed a two-run lead into the sixth when Bob Skinner turned the game around with a home run. "I thought I had him set up for a change," Craig said, shaking his head in despair. "He must have expected it."

Dick Stuart then reached out and pulled a low outside pitch for a base hit and marvelous Roberto Clemente hit a fast ball up the middle.

"It was where I wanted it," said Craig. "I'd been throwing him curves and sliders. I really thought I had him set up for a fast ball."

Once Upon a Time . . .

At that point Casey Stengel came out for a conference and decided to let Craig stay in the ball game. "That's what I did wrong today," the manager said.

Craig got behind on Smokey Burgess, gave up another hit, the second run, and set up the third as he departed.

"The whole game," Craig said, his long face somehow looking longer than usual, "all the way through, I felt I could shut them out. I felt strong, had good control. Ah, if we were hot and they were cold instead of the other way around I probably *would* have shut them out."

The winning run was set up when Don Zimmer couldn't quite locate Burgess's bunt in the eighth. This compounded things for the hot-tempered little third baseman. Although he was fielding poorly he was not hitting. He was 0 for 21 going in; coming out he was 0 for 24 and staring into his locker. "Even the goddam bunts are killing us," Zimmer said. "It's got to get you down after a while."

It is a distortion of history to believe, as some of the young Mets seem to these days, that the old Mets were clowns who expected—even wanted—to lose. They lost all right, and as Stengel once pointed out, "When you're losing, you commence to play stupid." But none of them wanted to lose.

This from Zimmer after the Mets had lost those first nine in a row: "There ain't nobody looking to lose in this game no matter how lousy you are."

And when, after two seasons in which he had managed to lose 46 games, a record, Craig was finally traded, he sighed with great relief. "Losing," Craig said. "I never liked to lose. I never even got used to it."

There were those who missed the developing mystique,

those who could find mundane rationales for the exquisite failures of the Mets. Cookie Lavagetto, the coach who had managed a bad Washington ball club, was one of them. "It's not luck," said Cookie, a man with a lined, used, terribly sad face. "It's limited ballplayers. I had it with Bob Lemon and Roy Sievers. They'd go first to third on us and then score on a pop fly. And you can't blame the players any more than you can change a leopard's spots."

And you know when he said that? He said that after the Mets had lost the first game of a doubleheader and seen a substantial lead erased in the third inning of the second game by, of all things, a snowstorm. On Palm Sunday. What does Cookie Lavagetto know about luck?

The Mets won their first game in Pittsburgh on April 23. "Ninety-nine more and we got the pennant," said Casey Stengel.

The score was 9–1 and Jay Hook, the mechanical engineer, was the winning pitcher.

"I'll tell you what I'm gonna do," Stengel shouted at Hook. "From now on I'm gonna let you pitch every day. You'll win 100 games. I win that I'll take the pennant."

Next to Hook, who not only started the big four-run second with a bases-loaded single, but pitched a relatively neat five-hitter, the big hero of the historic night was Elio Chacon. The soft-eyed little shortstop got three hits, was involved in all of the scoring, ran the bases with exciting recklessness and put a *joie de vivre* into the club so sadly lacking while he'd been nursing a series of injuries. It was not unnoticed by Stengel. "He looked," the manager said enthusiastically, "like he owned Venezuela."

"One and nine isn't a hell of a lot better than oh and ten," said Richie Ashburn, who must have known, be-

Once Upon a Time...

cause he played for the Phillies. "But it sure feels a lot better."

Before the night was over the Mets were actually reminding each other that Cincinnati had lost eight games in a row to start the previous season and then won the pennant.

The pitcher who won the first game for the New York Mets had a bachelor's degree from Northwestern and wore contact lenses. He was a central figure on the Mets both as a winner and a loser. He was young and seemingly effective. At the same time he was a failure at crucial moments. He was, then, almost by definition, a Met.

It had become fashionable around the Mets to blame Hook's failure on his refusal to knock hitters down. Weeks after Stengel had allowed him to take that terrible beating in Miami, the manager was saying "There was two outs. How'd I know he couldn't get the third one? I mean he had good control. He didn't knock anybody down, did he?"

What Stengel was saying was that he believed a pitcher who allowed five home runs to be hit off him should have at least become angry. He should have let a hitter or two know that he wasn't pitching for the fun of it. The approved method of doing that with a right-handed hitter is to aim one at his left ear.

"He looks like he ought to beat anyone," Stengel said of Hook. "If he pitched like Maglie nobody would beat him."

Sal Maglie, The Barber, was a notorious shaver of hitters. He beat people just by looking angry.

Hook would not pitch that way because he was not that kind of man. And when he was pressed he told of an experience he had as a high-school pitcher back in Grayslake, Illinois (pop. 3,000). He was pitching, it was getting dark, and the umpires were being stubborn about calling the game. "I hit a fellow in the head," Hook said. "He went to the hospital with a fractured skull. I didn't do it on purpose and I know he froze." He shrugged his high, wide shoulders helplessly. He meant he never wanted it to happen again, even by accident.

There are other pitchers who have this attitude. Unless they have overwhelming stuff, they never amount to anything.

The night after they won their first game, the Mets lost in Cincinnati 7–3. Craig Anderson was the losing pitcher. He lasted less than an inning. He had been counted on as a relief man. But he begged for a start and got it. "He don't look too much like a starter, does he?" Casey Stengel said.

No, but Charley Neal looked like Charley Neal. In that terrible first inning a ball hit by Vada Pinson scooted under Neal's glove for a two-base error that gave poor Anderson a shove toward the shower. Each day Neal gave more evidence of why the Dodgers had soured on him.

It was a cold and miserable day at the Polo Grounds and the Mets were down 15–5 with two out in the ninth. A fan stood in the aisle in right field, his shoulders hunched against the cold, his hands deep in his coat pockets. He jiggled up and down for warmth and all the time he was rooting. "C'mon," he said, almost to himself. "C'mon, one more run, just one more run."

"Why one more run?" he was asked.

Once Upon a Time . . .

"That would make it six," he said. "Then you could say if they got any pitching they woulda won."

The fan turned back toward Don Zimmer, who was at the plate. "C'mon," he said. "Just one more."

Zimmer popped up to the catcher.

The fan shrugged his shoulders. "Ah well," he said. "I'll be back tomorrow. No use giving up now."

Then there was the couple who were arrested behind home plate one night for committing what, considering the location, was an act of extraordinary friendliness. "But, officer," the woman protested, "we're married."

The Met fan of those days was not easy to understand, and the man who understood him least was George Weiss, the portly president. He had been general manager of the Yankees in their most successful years and knew so little about National League baseball in New York and the great hunger that had arisen for it since the year the Dodgers and Giants had defected that he thought no one would come to Mets games unless he assembled a lot of famous, if elderly, names. Thus he was in conflict much of the time with his friend Stengel, who wanted to go with "the youth of America." (Once, when Kanehl demanded to know why he wasn't in the lineup, Stengel snarled, "Because you're not old enough.")

Later on in the season, when the Mets were losing heavily and drawing well nevertheless, Weiss was asked if he understood what was happening. "No," he said. "I'm grateful, but I don't understand it."

It was, in fact, Weiss's impulse to prevent Met fans from exhibiting the banners that have now become such an intrinsic part of the Met scene. He relented, but M. Donald Grant, the former hotel room clerk who is

Leonard Shecter

Chairman of the Board of the Metropolitan Baseball Club, Inc., has picked up the Weiss gonfolon. Understand about Grant; he counts himself as a pretty good after-dinner speaker. He tells Pat-and-Mike stories—in dialect. Like about Pat, who had just been rapped on the nose with a shovel by Mike Clancy. "He had it in his hand and he let me have it," Pat moans.

"Didn't you have anything in your hands, Pat?"

"Only Mrs. Clancy."

And M. Donald Grant laughs and laughs.

Anyway Grant believes banners are O.K. as long as they're *positive* banners. When a fan exhibited a banner (B.C., before championship) which read "Welcome to Grant's Tomb," he was tossed out on his ear.

One of the few rules Stengel put down for his players was that there would be no card playing. It was his belief that card playing led to gambling, gambling led to losing, and losing led to resentments. Shortly after Harry Chiti, the ancient catcher, was obtained by the Mets, he went to Stengel during an airplane trip and asked for permission to start a gin-rummy game. Stengel said no. He suggested instead that if Chiti had nothing else to do he might go over the opposition hitters. Chiti went to sleep.

The most interesting thing about Chiti is that he was obtainer for "a player to be named later." When that player was finally named, it turned out to be Harry Chiti. Thus he was returned in payment for himself. There is no other reason for his fame.

An example of the underground railway Weiss was running. At the time Chiti came to the Mets, two other

Once Upon a Time . . .

arrivers were catcher Sammy Taylor and Dave Hillman, a pitcher. Taylor, twenty-nine at the time, was a no-hit first-string catcher for the Cubs who threatened to quit if he was not traded. He said he didn't get enough money to maintain two homes, in Chicago and South Carolina, where his wife preferred to live with their young daughter. His contract with the Cubs called for $12,000, which, considering he had four years in the majors, told something about his career.

Hillman, probably the only major-league pitcher to come out of Dungannon, Virginia, was thirty-five, and the most games he had ever won in a season was eight. He had been purchased from the Red Sox and held for delivery in Syracuse.

Bee Gee Smith was sent to the Cubs in payment for Taylor. To make room for Hillman and Chiti, Ginsberg and Labine were given releases. Ginsberg was philosophical about it. After all, when you were released by the Mets in those days it ought to have told you something. "I thought I had a good chance to stay," Ginsberg said. "But then I got off to a bad start and I knew they had to make a move. It's the perils of the trade."

Labine was less philosophical. He felt the Mets had no way of knowing whether he could pitch or not because they didn't look long enough. "I have the feeling I'm still a good pitcher or I wouldn't be here," he said. "It would be a funny thing if in one year you lose all you had. If I knew it was going to happen this way I never would have been here. I would have never left my business."

Regardless of their conflicting philosophies, Ginsberg and Labine were equally through with baseball. Nobody was picking up released Mets in those days.

It was in early May at a luncheon in Pittsburgh that Casey Stengel launched his "we want YOU for the Mets" campaign. The luncheon was in honor of Pirate manager Danny Murtaugh, but it was oversubscribed in honor of Casey Stengel. "This is a wonderful turnout, Casey," Murtaugh said. "I bet you didn't know people thought this much of old Dan."

When it came Stengel's turn to speak, he created the theme which, it can now be fairly said, culminated in 1969. Noting that there were several young college men in the audience and that the Pirates had a great team, a fine team with wonderful men at every position, Stengel said: "The Pirates are so good, how can you play for them? You can't. But you can play for the Mets. If you want rapid advancement, play for the Mets. We've got the bonus money. We'll even buy you a glove. So join us. Take the bonus money. Play a year or two. Then you can go back to school."

This is the way Casey Stengel turned on a generation.

Things were never dull around the Mets and, of course, one of the reasons was Casey Stengel. Traveling with him was like camping out with mummers. One should have had to pay for the privilege.

The old man let this one drop on the bus to the ball park on the Met's first trip to Cincinnati. The story went back to the days when he was playing right field for Pittsburgh.

"In those days," Stengel said, "when they got a new fire engine they liked to take it around so everybody in the city could see it."

Once Upon a Time . . .

So it was that the shiny engine was to be shown off at the ball park that day. In honor of the occasion, a mock house of two-by-fours was erected in center field. At the proper moment the house was set afire and the fire engine was supposed to dash out and douse the fire.

"Only they forgot to measure the bullpen entrance," Stengel recalled. "The engine was too big. They couldn't get it through."

The house flamed merrily and finally tumbled down upon itself. When it had burned to the ground—and still no fire engine—Stengel could stand it no longer. "I filled a glass with water in the dugout," he said, "and I ran out like Charlie Chaplin and—shoosh!—I threw the water on the fire. It was almost out, anyway. And you know something? The Fire Department was mad as hell at me."

It should not be forgotten that one of the people who contributed to the greatness of the Mets that first year was Gil Hodges. Hodges was hurt a lot and couldn't help a great deal. But he tried. One example: On May 4 of their first spring the Mets were behind 6–5 in the last of the ninth inning against Philadelphia. They loaded the bases with none out and excitement surged through the stands. Frank Thomas came up and popped up to the infield. Then Gil Hodges hit into a double play. Game over.

Said Hodges: "I thought Thomas would do it. When he didn't, I thought I would. I mean, I felt good up there. Sometimes you don't. Sometimes you feel wishy-washy. But I felt good."

One wonders whether Gil Hodges still remembers that time at bat.

Leonard Shecter

The way things were going for Don Zimmer, everybody knew he would soon be gone. It wasn't only that he was hitting so poorly, it was that he was such a good raconteur that he was too good to last.

One of his favorite stories was about his beaning in 1956.

"That was a great year for me," Zimmer said. "Pee Wee Reese wasn't going well and after the first month Walter Alston told me, 'You play.' My big chance. First ten AB's I got three hits. How much is that—.300, right? Then Hal Jeffcoat hit me right here." He pointed to a spot just under his left eye. He came close to losing the sight of it, didn't play again that season.

"That winter," he went on, "what the hell, I knew what I was going to get in my contract. The same thing I got last year. What else could they do? So when I got the contract from Buzzy Bavasi, I didn't even open it. I just tore it up, threw it away. After a while I got a letter from him. He said getting hit in the head must have made me goofy. 'What the hell's the matter with you?' he says in the letter."

Zimmer chuckled. "I ignored that one, too. Finally he called me up. So I told him: 'Hell, I hit .300' I think he was stunned for a minute, but only for a minute. Then he said 'Yeh, but you didn't drive in any runs.' "

When Zimmer stopped laughing, Bavasi asked him what he wanted. "A thousand," Zimmer told him. "Any year I hit .300 I want a thousand. I'll probably never do it again."

Bavasi sighed over the phone. "You're gonna get me fired," he said.

"But I got the thousand," Zimmer said.

Then Zimmer told about the time he got his biggest raise.

Once Upon a Time . . .

"We were kidding around, three of us," Zimmer said. "Buzzie, Ed Roebuck, and me. Roebuck told Buzzie he was going to have to give me $20,000. [Zimmer had made only $11,000 the season before.] I said 'Nah, that's too much.' I told him it'd make me feel like too good a ballplayer. Too much responsibility."

"Well, how much do you want?" Bavasi countered.

"Nineteen thousand," Zimmer answered, grinning.

"You know something?" Zimmer said. "I got it."

In a matter of days, Don Zimmer was traded to the Reds for Cliff Cook.

On May 9 the Mets picked up Marvelous Marv Throneberry from the Baltimore Orioles. George Weiss gleefully announced that he had managed to get Throneberry for cash, which was very hard to do. Throneberry was first called Marvelous when he was a young Yankee and it was believed, as it was about all young Yankees, that he was actually a marvelous ballplayer. He was something less.

When he came to the Mets he had a lifetime average of .238 and a reputation as a poor fielder. But as Weiss pointed out, "He has never had a chance to play regularly." The Mets gave him that chance. It revealed him.

Throneberry, twenty-nine at the time, looked older. He was thickly built and his bald head was covered with freckles. He was from a small town in Tennessee, chewed tobacco, and had a country accent.

Although he occasionally hit the long ball, he also hit into a lot of double plays and often struck out at crucial moments. On the field he was a disaster. Very quickly, he was being booed by the generally gentle Polo Grounds fans. He had become the personification of ineptitude. His first reaction, typical of ballplayers, was one of savage anger. Slowly though, with the help of Richie Ashburn, whose locker was next to his in the clubhouse, he came to understand his special role. There was the rainy night, for example, after he had had one of his routinely terrible games. He sat in his underwear in front of his locker and allowed a leak in the ceiling of the decrepit old clubhouse to drip, drip, drip, directly onto his bald head.

"I deserve it," he said.

"Yes, you do," said Richie Ashburn.

Richie Ashburn. The players called him White Mouse. He had very blond hair and deeply set blue eyes which often glinted with amusement. He found the world funny and the Mets hilarious. He was the first of the players to plug into the Met ambience, which was deadly serious on one level and a three-ring circus on another. There might never have been a Marvelous Marv Throneberry as we know and loved him if it had not been for Ashburn. Ashburn guided and goaded the slow-thinking Throneberry into a dim understanding, at least, of what the Mets were about.

Not only that, Ashburn was the Mets' best player. It's a trivia question winner. Did a Met hit over .300 in their first season? If so, which one? Right the first time.

Ashburn quit after the one year to go into television. It was the Mets' loss, and baseball's. But he was not the kind who stays in the game. He did it with natural ability and had only thinly disguised contempt for those who made it any other way. And when the ability was gone, Ashburn went with it.

Ashburn on baseball's most sacred fetish of keeping a book on hitters: "I think it's overrated. I mean, some guys like Hemus pay too much attention to it. I suppose

Once Upon a Time . . .

it's possible not to pay enough attention. But guys like Eddie Sawyer, Steve O'Neill, Charley Grimm, they practically never had a meeting.

"Meetings are all right if you got the ponies. It's all right to say, 'This guy can't hit a good fast ball.' But have you got a guy on your club who can throw a good fast ball? You tell a guy to pitch inside, outside. Fine, but how many pitchers have trouble just getting the ball over the plate?

"Sal Maglie used to pitch everybody the same way, fast balls up and in, breaking balls low and away. There wouldn't be any reason to have a meeting with a guy like that. Baseball is really a simple game. It's a game you have to play by ear."

Ashburn on managers who tell pitchers to knock hitters down: "All you do is get the hitter riled up. If a player didn't have courage he wouldn't put on a baseball suit. You're not going to scare him. How many times have you seen a guy get knocked down, get up and hit the ball out of the park? That throwing at people is overrated."

Ashburn on fighting ballplayers: "I always figured the guys who fight are guys who can't do anything else. You ever see Musial fight? Mays? Those guys never fight. But if you got a .220 lifetime batting average and you're not a good fielder, well you better do something. Me, I'd rather have a guy who can hit, run, and throw."

Ashburn on left-handed hitters: "A left-handed-hitting lineup can take you into a complete slump much easier than a right-handed-hitting lineup."

Ashburn on the squeeze play: "If you think your hitter is so bad he can't hit a fly ball, get another hitter."

They don't hardly make Mets like that anymore.

Leonard Shecter

There were many who felt that Cliff Cook was a much worse ballplayer than Throneberry. At first there was some wonder about why the Reds would give up a good hitter like Cook for a Casey Stengel putsie-downsie like Don Zimmer. Cook cleared this up in his first game when he got two hits, a triple and a single. He also made two gigantic errors at third base, just missed making a third, and got to several other batted balls too late to make an error or a play. The Mets lost the game to the Braves, 8–5.

"We got this man for hitting," Stengel commented.

Said Cook: "You don't know what goes wrong. You feel like you're looking right at the ball and all of a sudden—boom! But you can't let it get you down, can you?"

It wasn't all losing, of course. On May 21 the Mets had won nine of their last twelve games. They drew incredibly huge crowds to Dodger and Giant games. On June 7, to add to the merriment, Hobie Landrith was sent to Baltimore as part of what Weiss had declared a strictly cash payment for Throneberry. On this date, also, catcher Chris Cannizzaro was called up from the minor leagues. He was famous because Stengel called him Canzonarri, and, in moments of stress, Canzonarria.

By the end of June, things were back to normal and after a game in Pittsburgh which Marvelous Marv helped to throw away (the ball also took some funny bounces on the hard Pirate infield) Craig Anderson, the pitcher, was moved to remark: "Things are supposed to even out. But for us they never do."

It was along about this time that the Mets picked up Gene Woodling from the Washington Senators. They

Once Upon a Time . . .

paid $45,000 for him. He was thirty-nine years old.

"While this isn't altogether in keeping with our youth movement," George Weiss said, "our fans have supported us so well that we wanted to do something."

One of the things Casey Stengel scolded his pitchers about all the time was allowing opposition hitters to pull the ball down the lines and into the short porches. "Why wouldn't you want them to hit the ball to center field?" he would growl. "They're not going to hit it over a fence out there."

So on Sunday, June 17, in the first game of a doubleheader, Lou Brock, then of the Chicago Cubs, picked out a hanging curve thrown by Jackson and pickled it. The ball sailed more than 460 feet into the bleachers in right center field, scoring two runs.

"I was shocked," Casey Stengel said.

Actually this was one of the great days in Met history. For Brock's blast was the big blow in an inning in which the Cubs were able to score four runs at least partly because Marvelous Marv Throneberry couldn't get out of his own way. It was the first inning and Don Landrum led off with a walk. He was promptly picked off base by Jackson, but in the rundown Marvelous Marv managed to get himself charged with obstruction.

It was in the bottom half of that inning that Marvelous Marv hit his famous triple. He puffed into third obviously pleased with himself for having made up for his first inning gaffe and was promptly called out, on appeal, for having failed to step on first. When an irate and doubly shocked Stengel ran out to complain, the umpire told him to forget it. "He didn't touch second, either," the ump said.

Leonard Shecter

In the ninth inning of that game the Mets were behind 8–7 with two out and two on and Marvelous Marv was the hitter. He struck out.

The Mets lost the second game too, 4–3.

There were some days when the Mets just came out even. Like June 23, when they split a doubleheader with the Houstons (who were then called, ugh, the Colt 45's). In the first game Al Jackson pitched a wonderful one-hitter and even the infield rose to the occasion, turning in one of those once-in-a-while plays where the shortstop makes a great stop and, finding that he can't throw the ball to first, flips it to the second baseman who throws the runner out. It's at least as pretty as a triple play and Elio Chacon and Charley Neal pulled it on Hal Smith in the eighth inning.

"It was one of the best games you'll ever see pitched," said Stengel. "I thought he was marvelous. And one of the players said to me, 'Is he going in the second game?'"

Nine innings was the limit for Jackson. So Bob (Robert L.) Miller, who hadn't won a game in ten tries, strode out to the mound in the second game and it was as though the Mets had been transformed. The hits were virtually uncountable, the home runs a flood. The defense ran to six errors, three of them by Marvelous Marv Throneberry. And the final score was 16–3 in favor of the Houstons.

"You wouldn't think it was the same team, would you?"

No, but it was, it was.

Elio Chacon stopped a reporter near the batting cage in San Francisco one day. "Hey," he said, shyly. "You think we win today?"

The reporter, a gentle sort, said he was often disappointed, but he expected the Mets to win every day. Chacon nodded with satisfaction. "Well, we try every day," he said. "We try. That's *muy* important."

The Mets were beaten that day, twice, 11–4 and 10–3.

The Mets lost because of their pitching, hitting, fielding, and because they often had abysmal luck. They also lost because of umpires. That's what happens to bad teams. Take a game in late July. The Mets were losing to St. Louis, 6–4, in the ninth inning because they had made four errors, because of a two-out, bases-loaded, broken-bat blooper by the Cards' Ken Boyer, and because while Marvelous Marv was chasing Boyer in a rundown, Stan Musial was able to score, laughing. Still, in the last of the ninth, the Mets had the tying runs on base when Choo Choo Coleman, the little catcher Stengel was trying, and failing, to build up into another Yogi Berra, was caught in a rundown between third and home. In the course of the rundown, Coleman was clearly tripped by catcher Jim Shaffer while he was not in possession of the ball. Instead of awarding Coleman home plate (the way Landrum was awarded second because of Throneberry's interference not long before), Umpire Mel Steiner called him out and the game was over.

When Ed Bouchee made an error on the field and then struck out with two runners on base, Marvelous Marv walked up to him, looking angry, and said, "What are you trying to do, steal my fans?"

Then there was the time Ray Daviault, the pitcher, was having a bad day because of the fielders behind him.

Leonard Shecter

Every time he induced a hitter to hit a ground ball, somebody behind him would mess it up. At last after an inning in which he earned what should have been seven outs, Stengel trudged out to the mound and held out his hand for the baseball.

Daviault was upset. "I'm doing the job, Casey," he said. "What else can I do?"

"You could strike them out," Stengel said. "You know we can't catch grounders."

It was around this time, too, that Stengel, irritated with the fact that Frank Thomas often did not hit with men on base, confronted him and said, "if you want to be a sailor go join the Navy."

It was days before this pungent remark was translated. It turned out a company had offered a small yacht to the Met who hit its signs most during the season. The signs were located nearest the foul poles in left and right field, Polo Grounds home-run territory. Stengel's complaint was that in an effort to win the boat, Thomas was trying to pull the ball too much, thus not hitting it at all, especially with men on base. This was a base canard, of course. Thomas didn't want to be a sailor. He wanted to win the home-run title. And if he couldn't win it in the Polo Grounds, he couldn't win it anywhere.

On August 15, Al Jackson held the Philadelphia Phillies to one run for 14 innings. In the 15th, two runs scored when Tony Gonzales hit a sharp ground ball to first base. Although Marvelous Marv was there, when he put his glove down the ball just naturally jumped over it. Throneberry was not charged with an error. He had not, in fact, made an error in fifteen games.

Once Upon a Time . . .

He had a chance to make up for it all in the bottom of the 15th when he came up with runners on first and third. He struck out. "He ended up swinging on balls they was gonna walk him on," Stengel complained. After the Mets had lost for the ninety-second time, Richie Ashburn said, "They say it's easy to play on a loser. Hell it is. It's a lot easier to play on a winner. Seems to me I'm playing harder than I ever did before."

Other bad things were happening. Early on, to show they were stinting nothing in their drive for eventual excellence, the Mets signed Ed Kranepool out of James Monroe High School in the Bronx. They gave him a pot full of money and, amid high hopes, started him out in a Triple-A Syracuse. Soon he had to be dropped to Class A Knoxville. By August he was in Class D Auburn. The next season, playing with the Mets at the age of eighteen, Kranepool was greeted by a now famous banner: "IS KRANEPOOL OVER THE HILL?"

There were times, as the years went by, when many thought the Mets could have helped themselves simply by unloading Kranepool, what Branch Rickey, baseball's Mahatma, called addition by subtraction. Maybe so, but he was still there when the Mets won the pennant.

Marvelous Marv had a great September. He won several games with home runs and even started a couple of difficult, important first-to-second-to-first double plays. One day he helped beat the Dodgers with a home run and then made all three putouts in the ninth. Five kids came into the ball park one night, each dressed in a white T-shirt with a black letter inked on. "M-A-R-V" they spelled out. The fifth wore a "!" When

93

they climbed on top of the Mets' dugout and did a dance, they were thrown out of the park. So they bought their way back into the bleachers to see M-A-R-V!

Said Ashburn: "Throneberry is the people's choice and you know why? He typifies the Mets. He's either great or terrible." He paused and turned to Throneberry. "But you better not get too good," he said. "Just drop a pop fly once in a while."

Said Throneberry: "Aw, I haven't dropped a pop fly in a week."

Throneberry did so well at the last that he was the one who received the $7,000 power boat for hitting the outfield sign more than anybody else. Ashburn received a $5,000 power boat after a vote by fans and newspapermen. Throneberry soon found out that since Ashburn's boat was a gift it was not taxable, but that since he had won his in a contest, his was. Said Throneberry, scratching his bald dome and looking exquisitely unhappy, "I don't understand it."

At the end of that first season Ken MacKenzie, the Yale man, told some of the thoughts he had about the events of the year. MacKenzie: "When we started out this spring, I really thought we'd be all right, maybe even play .500 ball. I don't know what happened. Something happened, of course. You hear about clubs that win pennants. What happens is one guy picks up if another lets down. We've worked in reverse. We found a different way to lose every day.

"I don't think we were quite as bad as we looked. There was something this year that made every player a little worse than his potential. Our pitching, well, our pitching had a pattern. Error, base hit; error, base hit.

Once Upon a Time . . .

When you're pitching good ball and there's an error behind you, you bend your back and make the pitches. This is exactly what we didn't do. We probably set a record for unearned runs. That's no alibi for a pitcher, not when he's giving up the runs after the error."

The Mets finished with a 40–120 record. They had losing streaks of 9, 11, 13, and 17. Said Stengel: "Strangers are hard to manage. It was like spring training all year. But I expected to win more games. I was very much shocked."

Said Throneberry: "You think the fish will come out of the water to boo me this winter?"

The failures of George Weiss delighted many people, but none more than Bill Veeck, the man who owned the St. Louis Browns when Eddie Gaedel, the midget, was sent to the plate. Veeck delighted in saying that the Mets were the worst team ever assembled, worse even than his Brownies. He contended, noisily, that any team which had Bob Turley, Don Larsen, Roy Sievers, and Vic Wertz couldn't have been as bad as the Mets.

It turned out he was a prophet with honor. The Browns of 1953, former world's champion losers, lost 100 games in a 154-game schedule. The Mets lost 120 out of 160. Veeck didn't stop laughing until 1969.

Year II

The next year was the same, only more so. Delay of promised completion of Shea Stadium, the field named after Bill Shea, kept the Mets in the Polo Grounds all season. ("A chamber of horrors," Bobby Bragan, then manager of the Milwaukee Braves, called it.) The search for overage destroyers continued, George Weiss finally nailing down Duke Snider, thirty-six, for what he was willing to pay, a mere $40,000, ten thousand less if it turned out Snider couldn't play. It turned out he could, sort of, and for a while at least Snider lent a handsome gray-haired dignity to this terrible baseball team.

There was a newspaper strike in New York that lasted from December to April, and this enabled Weiss to practice a bit of his apparently inborn Machiavellianism. At first, every time Snider's name came up, Weiss said, "What's all this interest in old players?" Then, when he had succeeded in knocking down the price ("What does he want me to do?" Bavasi complained at one point, "pay Snider's salary?") he tried to keep the deal secret until the newspapers returned so he could get full value in publicity. Alas, he was outlasted by the strike.

There were deep changes in the Mets. A young fellow

named Ron Hunt was being noticed in training camp. He was the kind who always seemed to have a dirty uniform. Felix Mantilla, traded to Boston for Pumpsy Green (whose claim to fame was that he once got off a team bus with Gene Conley and set out for Israel, sort of) and Tracy Stallard (who was pitching when Roger Maris hit home run Number 61, which is even a greater claim to fame), told the world that leaving the Mets was like being "pardoned from the electric chair." He also said that the Mets were the worst team he had ever played on, including pick-up teams in Puerto Rico and Cuba. He may have been right, but one of the reasons they were so bad was the way Felix Mantilla played the infield.

Richie Ashburn had retired to broadcasting and the Mets were to start the season with an outfield, left to right, of Frank Thomas, Duke Snider and Ed Kranepool. Snider called it a classic. Gene Woodling, hired as playing coach, was summarily fired by Weiss for saying publicly that Marvelous Marv Throneberry deserved a raise rather than the salary cut Weiss had proffered. A knee operation on Hodges over the winter had him hobbling and ineffective. Another blow to the Mets was Chris Cannizzaro sticking his ring finger in front of a foul ball and suffering a severe dislocation fracture of the top joint. This left the catching up to Choo Choo Coleman, the sage of Orlando, Florida, who, employed as a sign painter in the road department over the winter, enjoyed pointing out the roadside signs he had created. (Choo Choo earned a bit of Metsiana glory when, after leaving the team for a while, he was asked by Charley Neal, "You remember me?" Coleman replied, "You number four."

For a while Stengel experimented with Elio Chacon in the outfield. The experiment was a failure. "What the

Once Upon a Time . . .

hell's the difference where you play him?" Stengel rasped. "He's still gonna knock in 27 runs for you." Or not enough for an outfielder.

Frank Thomas was a holdout for a week and accepted a $3,000 raise to $33,000. He had hit 34 home runs and knocked in 94 runs, and it was thought that Weiss had been unusually harsh with him. "No club has kept him more than one season since 1958," Weiss liked to point out. On the other hand, it was believed that all Weiss wanted to do was trade him, and it helped to keep his salary down. Thomas *was* traded, but not until the following season, to the Phillies. One of the first things he did in Philadelphia was get into a batting cage fight with Richie Allen. Naturally he was traded again. In 1965 he set a record even for Thomas. He played for three teams, the Phillies, Houstons, and Milwaukee, succeeding with none.

Salary dialogue between Johnny Murphy, Weiss' assistant, and Marvelous Marv Throneberry:

Throneberry: "People came to the park to holler at me, just like Mantle and Maris. I drew people to games."

Murphy: "You drove some away, too."

Throneberry: "I took a lot of abuse."

Murphy: "You brought most of it on yourself."

Throneberry: "I played in the most games of my career, 116."

Murphy: "But you didn't play well in any of them."

Some springtime assessments of the Mets by the Mets:

Charley Neal: "I know I'll be better. I've had two bad years in a row. I'd better be better. I'm sure guys like Craig, Jackson, and Hook aren't going to lose nineteen and twenty. I think we should win a lot more than the forty we won last year. Wasn't that awful?"

Rod Kanehl: "I think we have a faster ball club with a much better defense. The fact that many of the guys have been playing together for a year should be worth ten ball games right there. I'd say we ought to win twenty more than last year. I'm figuring them from the thirty-nine we lost by one run."

Roger Craig: "Sure we'll be better. How in hell could we be any worse?"

Gil Hodges: "Well, I'll tell you. Last year I predicted the Mets had a good shot at sixth place. I also predicted I'd have a good year—and I wound up twice in the hospital. What could I possibly say now that the people would believe?"

The Mets beat the Yankees 1–0 in St. Petersburg, Craig and Jackson sharing the shutout. Stengel was genuinely grateful. "You fellas play 154 games like that and you'll win the World Series," he told them. "If you want the money in advance, just write me a letter and I'll give it to you now."

Before Hunt was able to break into the Met infield, it consisted of Al Moran at shortstop, Larry Burright at second base and Charley Neal at third. ("Neal plays third base like it was a joke," said Stengel.) With those stalwart men in operation the Mets built up an 8–5 spring record that actually led the Citrus League, NL division. Stengel said he thought it would be too cold for a parade in New York at that time of year.

On April 4 it was discovered that Frank Thomas wasn't

Once Upon a Time . . .

playing because of a bad elbow, an injury which the Mets had been trying to hide. Stengel was asked why, and his answer, since it was the truth, was the kind that drove Weiss up the wall. "Because maybe I want to sell him," Stengel said.

On this date, too, the Mets returned Wynn Hawkins, a pitcher, to Cleveland. In 12 and ⅔ innings he had an ERA of 1.42. He had given up only one walk and no home runs. If the Mets had kept him they would have to pay the Indians $35,000. Weiss said that had nothing to do with it. Nobody believed him. He said that was terribly unfair. And perhaps he was right. What did Wynn Hawkins ever do?

Louie Kleppel, a short, heavy, disreputable-looking baseball fan with a voice that could scatter pigeons a mile away, was one of the Mets' biggest fans and severest critics. He sat in the Polo Grounds bleachers near the runway to the clubhouse and cogently criticized the players as they entered and exited. To incur the displeasure of Louie Kleppel was to make the trip to and from the clubhouse an agonizing, noisy, and humiliating experience. The players hated him. But it is possible he made them try harder.

Still, in the spring of 1963 even Louie Kleppel was optimistic. "I sat through seventy of their games last year," Louie said. "It got so some of the players looked like they were apologizing for winning. This year it's different. This year we have some ballplayers."

Maybe so. But vendors in St. Petersburg were having trouble selling autographed rockets for $2.75. "You'll be sorry," one of them cried, "when they win the championship."

Leonard Shecter

Anybody want to buy a rocket autographed by the 1963 springtime Mets?

When the Mets returned to the Polo Grounds to play the Cardinals on Opening Day, the fans were already in mid-season form. One of their banners read: "BRING BACK BUTTERBALL BOTZ."

The Mets lost the opener 8–0. After the game Casey Stengel stormed into his tiny office, slammed his baseball cap down on the desk and announced: "The attendance was robbed. We're still a fraud."

"I know we're better than we looked today," said Ed Kranepool. "It's too bad, we wanted so much to play good."

That's what comes out of signing for $85,000 right out of high school and foregoing a college education. Bad grammar.

George Weiss didn't like the idea of Stengel throwing young Kranepool, who was by heavy-hipped build and unskilled inclination a first baseman, into the outfield. This was Stengel's argument: "The front office tells you, why do you want to put a young fellow out there and ruin him? But they don't tell you the other guy [Throneberry] is gonna ruin you too."

The Mets lost the second game of the season too, being shut out again 4–0. They had come north with a team designed to keep the opposition from scoring runs. It was conceded that the Mets themselves would not score many. But this was ridiculous.

Not only that, the defense of the defensive Mets was showing holes. Tim Harkness at first base had a ball bounce off his chest, absolutely destroyed a pop foul, and generally played his position as though he carried a Marvelous Marv virus. As one churlish Met fan remarked, "Might as well have Marvelous Marv in there. He'll hit better."

Al Jackson was the Met pitcher in that game. "A game like today," he said, "it just happens. It's gonna happen sometimes. But it's not gonna happen always. I mean you don't think we're gonna get shut out all year, do you?"

No. In their third game Duke Snider hit a home run in the second inning, ending the shutout streak. The Mets lost, 6–1.

The Mets didn't match their first-year opening losing streak of nine. After losing eight straight they beat the Milwaukee Braves 5–4 on Ron Hunt's ninth-inning double. Mrs. Payson was so delighted she sent flowers to the Hunt household. It was the worst thing she could have done. Ron Hunt was allergic to flowers.

Some quotes from Marvelous Marv Throneberry, who wasn't playing.

On Choo Choo Coleman: " 'Hey Bub,' is about the only thing I've ever heard him say. But he says it nice."

On positive thinking: "What the hell is positive thinking? What good does it do you to think you're going to do something when you know damn well you're not?"

Throneberry didn't make his outfield debut until May

Leonard Shecter

1, or Mayday as it's called in the Air Force. This was not exactly a Stengel capitulation, for Kranepool was in left, Snider in center, and Throneberry in right. It was, press box enthusiasts suggested, the best defensive alignment since General Custer's.

In honor of the occasion the "Star-Spangled Banner" record was played at the wrong speed. "I thought," said Throneberry, who by this time thoroughly understood his role as a Met, "they would dedicate it to me."

The first batter, Johnny Temple of the Houstons, hit the ball toward Throneberry.

"A lot of people think I've played in the outfield a lot," Throneberry was to say later. "I never played but about half a dozen games out there. And this spring I never played anywhere. It's tough. I saw that ball coming and I said to myself, 'Oh God, what do I do now?'"

What he did was fall down. The ball bounced in front of him and when it changed direction on the lumpy, wet outfield, and he attempted to move with it, his legs went out from under him. He took a long, sliding flop on the back of his nice new white knickerbockers. It was Throneberry at his best.

Snider ran up to lend a hand, but all he could do was laugh. He looked down at Throneberry, put his hands on his hips and laughed. "If it was Ashburn, he would have yelled 'Safe!'" Throneberry said.

"I was laughing so hard I could barely get enough breath to tell him to throw the ball to second." Snider said. "He made a hell of a throw."

It was such a good throw it held Temple to a double on the single.

As if things weren't bad enough, this was the year of

the balk. And like most everything else—the weather, the cost of living, and George Weiss's dyspepsia—this somehow worked against the Mets. It all started because Walter O'Malley, the president of the Dodgers (and, some insisted, undercover president of the National League) had a player named Maury Wills on his team. Wills stole bases for a living and it occurred to O'Malley that Wills might find it easier to steal if pitchers were forced to obey a rule on the books which required them to come to a full one-second pause at the end of their windup. Umpires had long required that there be some sort of pause, but it had become a sort of sliding pause.

At any rate, O'Malley dropped a hint to Warren Giles, the president of the league who sneezed when O'Malley caught cold, and Giles let his umpires know he wanted them to enforce the rule. Now umpires are a special breed of men. They tell people what to do. They don't like to be told. So they pulled the classic umpire ploy. They overenforced. They called four, five, seven balks a game. As Stengel was to say many times, they were making a goddam joke out of the game.

Eventually the umpires killed the balk enforcement with kindness. In the meantime, the Mets got stiffed. Take a game in Philadelphia, April 22. Four balks were called against the Mets, three of them against a rookie named Don Rowe. In short order the Phillies had an 8–3 lead. Part of it was due to poor pitching, of course, but part of it was that the balk calls upset the kid to the point where he didn't know where to put his feet anymore, much less how to throw strikes. The other part of it was that as soon as he had a man on first he had a man on second, courtesy of the plate umpire.

To make it worse, the Mets came through with one of

their exciting fall-short finishes. Frank Thomas hit a two-run homer to start the ninth. Then the Mets scored another, to make it 8–6, promptly loaded the bases, and a couple of knots of hopeful Met fans, who had come down to Philly for the occasion, were wandering around grumbling, "Let's go Mets."

This time, though Rod Kanehl was not equal to the occasion. He struck out. But if it hadn't been for those called balks . . .

The fans remained great and loyal. After the Mets returned late one night after three straight losses to the Pittsburgh Pirates, there were 200 cheering fans at the airport. One of them carried a sign which read: "IN SPITE OF IT ALL, WE LOVE THE METS."

The improved Met infield, with Hunt at second and Al Moran at shortstop, was serving a purpose. It was, for one thing, making the pitchers more comfortable. The year before, a pitcher went to the mound, looked behind him and there were Elio Chacon and Felix Mantilla. So they laughed. It was either that or cry.

The way the game of baseball is supposed to be played, a pitcher tries to get a hitter to hit the ball on the ground. He then has reasonable expectations that his fielders will come up with the ball and turn it into an out. Coming up with the ball was, early on, precisely the Mets' difficulty. Some people thought this charming. But it gave the pitchers sore arms.

Now though, things had changed. "There is a definite difference this year," Ken MacKenzie said one fine day in May. The self-confessed lowest-paid member of the

Once Upon a Time . . .

Yale class of '56 put it this way: "My attitude reflects that of the whole club. It's a matter of confidence. I feel like a better pitcher, that I have more of a chance."

Of course, it was possible that MacKenzie had, at age twenty-nine, suddenly become a better pitcher. But he doubted it. The difference for pitchers was turning around and seeing Ron Hunt and Al Moran rather than Elio Chacon and Felix Mantilla.

At the same time, the fact that the Mets were slightly better was itself a cause of discord. Because now, instead of losing 12–5, they lost 3–2. Very frustrating.

Take two losses to the Braves in Milwaukee. The first one was by 3–2. There was some agonized grumbling among the faithful that maybe Casey Stengel was losing his grip. Instead of bringing in Galen Cisco, who was beaten late, he should have brought in Larry Bearnarth, the kid who had the guts of a burglar. The next day, with the bases loaded in the tenth, the kid with the guts of a burglar gave up the hit that beat the Mets 11–9.

To many Metsophiles, Larry Bearnarth represented the new wave. He was young and tough and fearless and convinced he could win. He never was a big winner with the Mets and this may have been because he was never quite good enough as a pitcher. It may also have been that the Mets were never good enough for him.

But Stengel loved him. The reason was simple. The first time Larry Bearnarth got into a baseball game for the Mets he hit Dick Lynch, Cincinnati pinch-hitter extraordinary, plunk, right in the kidney. The Bear, as he came to be called, had given up two hits and there were runners on second and third when Lynch came up. "I figured I could walk him and set up the force," Bearnarth said. "I also knew I'd better pitch close to him. So I figured I'd just as well hit him."

Stengel was so delighted he did a dance in the dugout.

Stengel went a long way with the kid, longer than the front office wanted him to. He was always a loyal man. Up to a point, of course. Eventually, he always bowed to the baseball decision. No matter what the Mets actually did, Casey Stengel was always trying to win.

Not, of course, that he was ever inflexible. Carlton Willey, the brooding, taciturn, gentlemanly man from Cherryfield, Maine, who in moments of stress might release a strong "golly," was one of Stengel's favorites for a while. He was a favorite because he won nine games for the Mets in 1963, which was a lot. But he was not Stengel's kind of pitcher. Unlike Bearnarth, he never hit anybody, not purposely anyway. Indeed, he once described the beginning of the end of his career with Milwaukee this way: "It was in the first inning of the second game of a doubleheader. We were playing the San Francisco Giants. With one out and two runs in on Willie Mays' home run, Birdie Tebbetts [the manager] signaled for me to knock down Orlando Cepeda. I wouldn't. I couldn't. I struck Cepeda out, but I was really chewed out at the end of the inning.

"I gave up a walk and a hit in the second inning and I was out of there. It was almost three weeks later that I got my second chance. I wound up pitching only 73 innings."

There were qualities to the Polo Grounds that will never be duplicated. The clubhouse was at one end of the field, and up a flight of steps. After a while Met fans dis-

Once Upon a Time . . .

covered that they could gather below the clubhouse windows, chant the name of today's hero—and despite the losing there was often a hero of sorts—and demand that he come out and take a bow. Thus there was the game in which a home run by Choo Choo Coleman broke up a 12–12 tie (a perfect example of the sort of messy game the Mets could become involved in) and 500 fans gathered below the clubhouse chanting, "We want Choo Choo." He had to pull his trousers back on and go outside and wave, like Il Duce from a Roman balcony. "It's nice," Choo Choo said.

Many other Mets got calls to the balcony—Casey Stengel, Marvelous Marv, Richie Ashburn, Ron Hunt. And the inarticulate Choo Choo had said it best after all. It *was* nice.

Another thing about the Polo Grounds. It was a place where "Days" were given to opposition ballplayers. With no tradition of their own, the Mets invited old Dodgers, Giants, and Yankees on Old-Timers' days. And they staged "Days" for players like Willie Mays. His Day in 1963 drew 49,431 customers and he received a truckful of loot, including a seven-foot salami.

It wasn't just the Days that drew the people, though. Mays' Day was on Saturday. Sunday, 53,880 showed up. In honor of the occasion the Mets beat the Giants 4–2.

Among the bedsheet banners that appeared at the Polo Grounds were:

THE METS AIN'T FIRST
'TIS SAD BUT TRUE
BUT DEAR OLD METS
WE LOVE YOU

GO MRS. PAYSON, GO

LET'S GO STENGEL LANCERS

Leonard Shecter

And one day after the Mets had blown one of their seven-hour doubleheaders, 8–7 and 10–4, a fan was heard to remark: "One thing you got to admit—they give you your money's worth."

While he was still a Met, Richie Ashburn had this to say about umpires: "They're cheating us because we're horseshit and they know it." He was quite correct. Close decisions seemed to go against the Mets all the time. It wasn't as though umpires were mean and narrow enough to think that it didn't matter to the Mets if they lost. Like where were they going? No self-respecting umpire would feel that way, would he? Of course not. So it was entirely accidental that Joe Amalfitano of the San Francisco Giants was able to beat the Mets with a foul home run, 4–3, in the eleventh inning. We know it was foul because everybody could see that it missed the foul pole by inches. But there was a foot-wide screen on the foul pole—in fair territory.

After the game Roger Craig, who was pitching at the time, pounded on the door of the umpires' dressing room and called them terrible names. The worst he reserved for Frank Walsh, who made the call.

Then Craig said: "All the names I've called you, if you had any guts you'd come out." Not that Craig was much of a fighter. It's just that losing got frustrating. Even for a Met.

For the sake of history, it should be remembered that the Mets didn't lose all those games because of umpires. For some reason they were particularly terrible against the Houstons. They were even bad against them in 1969. On this evening in Houston in May of 1963 they lost the game because

Once Upon a Time . . .

(1) In the second inning Ron Hunt, playing third base, ranged far out of his position attempting to stop a ground ball, thus preventing the shortstop from making a play and letting the man get on.

(2) Larry Burright, at second, was the middle man on a double play. That is, he should have been the middle man on a double play. He did a lot of things, among them knock the ball down as though it were a mosquito. But he did not make the double play.

(3) Tim Harkness dropped a routine throw at first base.

(4) Norm Sherry, the catcher, enabled a man who apparently was not going to hit the ball to reach first base by interfering with his swing.

(5) Jim Hickman set himself in the outfield to catch a line drive. He focused his keen eye on the ball and watched it sail past him. Some say it was ten feet away, but it couldn't have been more than five.

"Cheez, that was a poor game," Casey Stengel said.

By the end of May, it had become apparent that Al Moran wasn't going to make it at shortstop. Also, he was hitting .184. This was not noticeable because Frank Thomas was hitting .196, Choo Choo Coleman was hitting .182, Cliff Cook .131, Rod Kanehl .133, and Norm Sherry .106. Pretty soon Sherry's batting average was down to .088. It was, as one fan remarked, the most improved tenth-place team in history.

At a press conference in Los Angeles late in May, George Weiss wiped away a tear and allowed as how he still didn't understand what was going on with the Mets. Everywhere he went, Weiss said, he found interest in the Mets positively staggering. "You don't know how it happened, but you're happy it did," Weiss said. "You're just eternally grateful."

But it turned out that, secretly, Weiss did rather think he knew what happened. He thought it was a tribute to all the money he'd been spending to weld the Mets into a fighting organization. Why he had spent $400,000 with the Milwaukee Braves alone and he broke it down this way: $150,000 for Felix Mantilla and John DeMerit; $130,000 for Frank Thomas; $30,000 for Ken MacKenzie; $50,000 for Ron Hunt; $40,000 for Carlton Willey and $5,000 for a look at Butterball Botz. If it hadn't been for Willey and Hunt, Weiss could have hollered to the cops that he was robbed.

Actually, the only thing Weiss was right about was Casey Stengel. "I think the biggest thing that Casey has done is that even last year the club didn't quit," Weiss said. "That is a greater mark of ability even than winning a pennant by eleven games."

Marven Eugene Throneberry, the man whose initials were M.E.T., had the can tied to him by the Mets on May 9. The Met front office, spelled Weiss, and dotted with a Johnny Murphy, a friendly sort who looked as though he wore suspenders *and* a belt, never understood Marvelous Marv Throneberry and what he meant to the Mets. Just as they didn't understand why huge crowds fought their way into a crumbling, obsolete ball park to cheer for a losing team; just as Mrs. Payson went off to Europe with instructions that only winning scores be relayed to her; just as George Weiss went blindly on shuffling players like a losing card player shuffles cards after all the other gamblers have left, so it was that Marvelous Marv Throneberry was sent off to Buffalo in

Once Upon a Time . . .

order to make room for some nonentity who could never carry Marv's marvelous glove.

There were objections, of course. Bedsheet banners read: "BRING BACK MARVELOUS MARV." The New York *Post* printed a daily account of Marvelous Marv's activities in Buffalo. It was all to no avail. Marvelous Marv didn't even have the good sense or grace to play spectacularly poorly in Buffalo; he played just poorly enough to avoid being recalled. He was that kind of player.

Nowadays Marvelous Marv Throneberry comes back for Old-Timers' games. As time goes by he is less and less able to kid himself about the old days. He prefers to remember his days as a Yankee. Like George Weiss, Throneberry always overestimated his ability.

Then there were the gentle, kind, sweet things that happened. Like Don Drysdale throwing Duke Snider a "cookie."

It was in Los Angeles, before the game, as it happened, that a reporter asked Drysdale if it might occur to him, under the proper conditions, to sort of let his old gray friend Duke Snider, well, maybe, perhaps, swing at an easy pitch to hit. "You mean," Drysdale said, his eyes dancing with merriment, "throw him a cookie?" Drysdale said this was against the very nature of a pitcher, especially one so tough and mean as he.

But in the game, once the Dodgers had a big lead, Drysdale did indeed serve up a cookie. Snider hit it over the right-field wall.

Drysdale, of course, denied all. "I just wanted to see if he could still hit the high fast ball," Drysdale said. He couldn't conceal a most attractive boyish grin. "He can."

Leonard Shecter

And this bit of sweetness from Casey Stengel on Frank Thomas, who was suffering several little ills: "I wouldn't want him to die because I couldn't get anything for his body right now."

Then came Jimmy Piersall. His time with the Mets was brief, peripatetic, and not as amusing as some like to remember. It was said of Piersall that he could never replace Marvelous Marv. He had too much talent. But Piersall's major talent at that late stage of his career, it turned out, was for invective.

At first, all was beautiful, if not exactly serene. When he arrived at the Mets, Piersall made claims to having been born a Met, a distinction normally reserved for Marvelous Marv and certain experienced losers among their fans. He was happy to be a Met, Piersall said, delighted to be playing for Casey Stengel. "He's the guy who gave me my start," Piersall said. "In 1953 he selected me as the best defensive right fielder he ever saw and he had Hank Bauer playing for him. He picked me for two All-Star teams. He always went out of his way to talk to me."

And so, it was thought, a new delight was being added to the Mets. It was, after all, Piersall who once pulled out a water pistol and squirted an umpire after an argument at the plate. It was Piersall who used to sit down with his back against the center-field monument in Yankee Stadium and take a snooze during pitching changes. It was Piersall who used to play center field directly behind second base and defy Billy Martin of the Yankees to hit a ball over his head.

And it was of Jimmy Piersall that Casey Stengel said: "I ain't worried about all that. I can always fire him."

The Mets were in such bedraggled condition that Pier-

Once Upon a Time . . .

sall, by definition just another overage destroyer, helped for a while. He was, even then, a good fielder. But he simply could not hit and his batting average disappeared into the maw of the Mets' under-.200 club. One thing he did do, as promised, was run around the bases backward when he hit his 100th home run. Stengel didn't mind. "He didn't run to third base first, did he?" said the old man. Well, no, and since Stengel was, after all, the man who had once released a bird from under his cap as a salute to an umpire, all seemed well.

In the end, though, Piersall couldn't even make it with the Mets. He couldn't hit enough and he was, as Stengel liked to say, fired.

Marvelous Marv went quietly. Piersall went kicking and screaming. He seized every opportunity to attack Casey Stengel, the man who had given him his start. The old man was too old. He was befuddled. He fell asleep on the bench. If it weren't for Stengel the Mets would finish ninth, or eighth, or fourth.

Piersall formed a cabal with broadcaster Howard Cosell, a man Casey Stengel refused to view as anything more or less than an irritating electronic device, to denigrate Stengel at every opportunity. It was an unworthy, unsuccessful effort. In the end, only a broken hip moved Stengel out. What moved Piersall out was something that never affected Stengel—fading talent.

In an effort to jump on the Met bandwagon, the New York *Post* ran what it called a "Let's Go Mets" contest. It was a simple-minded thing and unworthy of mention, except that I wrote an article in the *Post* as a tongue-in-cheek aid to those entering the contest. It was no aid,

Leonard Shecter

of course, but did illuminate some of the thinking of the thinking man's Met fan.

The story went:

"As a public service (and also as a sort of tip sheet for those who enter the New York Post's Let's Go Mets contest) here is a list of outstanding qualities and the Mets who have them.

"Best outfielder: Jimmy Piersall. He was the best Met outfielder while he was still with Washington. Then again, Duke Snider was the best Met outfielder while he was still with Brooklyn.

"Best-hitting outfielder: Duke Snider. What this means is he *should* be the best-hitting outfielder. In the meanwhile, if you mention his batting average, he blushes.

"Best infielder: Ron Hunt. This kid has everything going for him including an urge to cripple the opposition. He's a credit to the Milwaukee organization and a living tribute to its stupidity.

"Best-hitting infielder: Ron Hunt.

"Best Met: Ron Hunt.

"Toughest competitor: Ron Hunt. When he tags anybody he leaves a black-and-blue mark. He ought to have a great season if somebody doesn't ram a set of spikes down his throat. And where does all this leave Charley Neal? In a slump.

"Best pitcher: Al Jackson. Jackson is also the Mets' second-best pitcher. The Mets talk about building around him for the future. By then he'll be too old to do them any good. They ought to trade him for half a ball club. But they won't. Too slick.

"Best catcher: Norm Sherry. Has a small problem.

Once Upon a Time . . .

His brother, who is a pitcher, outhits him. Comes the revolution, and the wealth will be divided more equitably.

"Cutest Met: Choo Choo Coleman.

"Most dignified-looking Met: Duke Snider. That gray hair gets them. If he offered to sell you the Brooklyn Bridge you'd be certain he owned it.

"Most dignified Met: Carlton Willey. He'll never say anything harsher than 'golly sakes.'

"Handsomest Met (senior division): Duke Snider. That gray hair again. Plus those baby-blue eyes. If you're a woman, after he's sold you the Brooklyn Bridge, you'd want to cuddle him.

"Handsomest Met (bobby-sox division): Larry Bearnarth. May also be best of college-type dressers. Now if he could only pitch.

"Friendliest Met: Rod Kanehl. If you had as little talent as he you'd be friendly too. Also you'd bust your tail on the field. That's why he's Casey Stengel's favorite Met.

"Richest Met: Ed Kranepool. He got a large bonus and hasn't had much chance to spend it. He's only 18 and wouldn't know how to spend it anyway.

"Funniest Met: Don Rowe. Get him to tell you about his dream team with Pffft Pfoffenberger leading off. Pfoffenberger is so fast that when he hits a ground ball you don't throw it to first, you throw it to third.

"Fastest base runner: Choo Choo Coleman. Almost as fast as Pfoffenberger, which is very fast for a catcher. Only there's one thing in the game he hasn't quite learned. How to get on first.

"Most intelligent Met (science division): Jay Hook. Excellent on principles of pitching. Not so good on practice.

"Most intelligent Met (arts division): Larry Bearnarth. Active seeker after things cultural. Even got Kranepool to stop sitting around in lobbies.

"Nicest man on the Mets: Carlton Willey.

"Least talkative: Any time you want ten minutes of silence get Choo Choo Coleman, Al Moran, and Galen Cisco to conduct a seminar on any topic.

"Best all-around Met: Casey Stengel. Without him this collection would fall apart like a saltine under frozen butter. Without him there would be no Mets. There might not even be a world."

As the June 15 trading deadline approached, Roger Craig began to get sweaty palms. He wanted to be traded so badly it was keeping him awake at night. Not that he didn't love the Mets, understand. It was just that he had once been spoiled by being on a winner. Losing twenty-four games, as he had in that first season, was sheer purgatory. What he really wanted was to go home to the Dodgers, but he was willing to settle for less—say twelve losses with the St. Louis Cardinals.

On the eve of the trade deadline it happened that the Mets beat the Reds in Cincinnati. The score was a thumping 10–3. (Any winning Met score thumped.) It also happened that Craig had come into the game in relief of Carlton Willey, who had a line drive hit off his shin which raised a lump about the size of those which graced the lumpy legs of Casey Stengel.

Instead of savoring his save, Craig wanted to talk trade. "There are a few clubs that want to get me," he said, "but our club wants too much. You can understand a contender not wanting to give up somebody who's helping them."

Once Upon a Time . . .

So Craig looked around and decided it would have to be the Dodgers' Moose Skowron for Roger Craig. The only place the deal was made was in his dreams.

It was in this game that Duke Snider hit the 400th home run of his career and, like Craig, he was unhappy. Not about leaving the Dodgers, where he hadn't been playing. And not about not being traded to the Yankees, which he had been looking forward to. (He learned to dig the Mets right off.) No, he was unhappy about his batting average. "It's sickening to look at that scoreboard when I come up to the plate and see .220. It's embarrassing."

But like a lot of other Mets, he got used to it.

What with the injury to Willey, Craig's crabbiness, and Snider's 400th home run, no one paid any attention to Casey Stengel. The old man sat there for a while in the little clubhouse, taking in the scene. Finally he could stand it no longer. "Hey," he yelled suddenly. "I got hit in the leg too." He pointed to the lumps on his own old wheels. And when this didn't get more than a brief little laugh, he hardened his eyes, pointed at Snider and said, "When you get through talking, go over to the other clubhouse. You've been traded to the Reds."

Sample of Jimmy Piersall humor in a remark to Frank Thomas. "You helped the team today, Frank. You hurt your leg."

One of the frustrations of being a Met fan was that they gave you a bellyache. Not because of all the losing. One gets used to that and, possibly, in some perverse way, begins to enjoy it. The bellyaches came from caring about individual Mets; not the clowns, but the players you knew were better than their records. Like Jay Hook. He was 8–19 in 1962, with a 4.84 ERA. Things had to get better for him the next season. He had all the equipment. So what if he wouldn't throw at hitters? Willey didn't throw at hitters and *he* won.

But nothing got better. The better Hook pitched, the better the hitters seemed to hit him. At one point he beat the Cubs with a two-hitter and it was decided his only problem was that he tried too hard, that if he just threw naturally and easily there was great spin on the ball and it moved beautifully, which is to say it arrived quickly, doing unexpected things. The very next time out, though, he gave up six smoke-trailing hits in less than two innings and was right back where he started. "He drives you crazy," said Ernie White, the pitching coach. "He has as much stuff as anybody in the league and he drives you crazy."

They hit everything he threw—fast ball, curve, change; everything but the slider, which he had been told to shove up his anemometer. Hook decided his problem was that his strikes were just too good. Others thought that his pitches were being read, because the hitters were so eager to come to bat they were running up to the plate. ("It was the umpire who had our signs," Stengel growled. "Every time he threw a pitch the umpire said 'ball four.' ") And Larry Bearnarth, the young upstart, said, "Did you see the hitters? They were like this." He struck a batting pose and ground his back foot hard into the floor. This is the baseball sign for digging in, which a pitcher isn't supposed to let a hitter do. "You got to knock them down once in a while," Bearnarth said.

He was to learn, though, that knocking them down wasn't enough. You had to be able to pitch. Bearnarth

Once Upon a Time . . .

tried like hell, just like Hook. In the end, though, they both came up short. And Bearnarth gave a lot of bellyaches, too.

A lot of funny things happened at Yankee Stadium on the night of June 24, 1963. For one thing the Mets beat the Yankees 6–2, in an exhibition game attended by so many that the Yankee brass was shaking its head in amazement. For another, the fans, Met fans mostly, were so exuberant, they tore up the Stadium somewhat. Commented Ralph Houk (still a winner and very Yankee in those days and thus somewhat uptight): "It wasn't too bad. The Battle of the Bulge was worse."

He didn't know how bad things were. A fan named Jim DelVecchio had it worse. DelVecchio, twenty-four years old, a color technician, father of one with another on the way, lived in the Bronx, and was a Yankee fan.

As he told the story, DelVecchio, who came to perhaps twenty Yankee games a year, arrived early in the evening, bright-eyed and bushy-tailed with a friend and a married couple, all three of them Met fans. Naturally they had come with hand-lettered signs intended to encourage the Mets to great feats of derring-do.

But so had DelVecchio. And his sign read: "I'M A YANKEE FAN".

"I knew the New Breed [which was what some newspapers were calling the Met fans] would be up there with a lot of Met signs. So I brought a Yankee sign," DelVecchio said.

He and his friend, however, were met at the gate by a Yankee house cop who refused them admission unless they checked the signs. They also checked a pint of whiskey.

Leonard Shecter

"We didn't have to check the whiskey," he said. "They didn't frisk us. We could have hid it. But we thought what the heck, we could buy all the beer we needed. So we checked it."

It was an upsetting experience. "I have this Yankee hat," DelVecchio said. He held out a gaudy straw job with "YANKEES" emblazoned on the blue band and assorted buttons which proclaimed his loyalty to Dan Topping's money factory. "After what happened I was ashamed of it. I threw it under my seat."

That wasn't the half of it. After the Mets had ruined what was left of his evening by beating the Yankees, he went to get his signs and booze back. He was told they weren't there.

"I really used to like the Yankees," DelVecchio said. "I thought winning was everything. Now I'm finding out it ain't."

DelVecchio wasn't the only friend the Yankees lost that night. They prepared for the crowd as though a war were scheduled. The banners which were smuggled in under shirts (most of them said "METS SI, YANKEES NO") were quickly seized and destroyed by house cops. The Yankee explanation was that banners blocked the view of people. They had a policy. It was established by George Weiss, who by then was, of course, with the Mets. It had to be a joke somebody up there was playing.

All this has changed now. Dan Topping is gone and CBS owns the Yankees. Mike Burke, who is the president of the club, welcomes banners. It will, nevertheless, be years before the Yankees catch up to the Mets. Maybe they never will.

On June 20 the Mets lost a game to the Cards because,

Once Upon a Time . . .

Rod Kanehl said, "I blew a routine triple play." He really did.

Tim Harkness, a curly-haired, reedy young man with immense grey eyes, hit a bases-loaded home run for the Mets against the Cubs in the fourteenth inning at the Polo Grounds on June 27. There were two outs at the time, the Mets were behind two runs and the count was three and two on him.

The Mets won, 8–6. This is what Harkness said after he came into the clubhouse, had gone back to the door to do the balcony scene for the "we want Harkness" fans, and returned to the stool in front of his locker.

"I couldn't believe it was me hit that. It doesn't seem like good things happen to me. When I hit the ball it didn't even make my heart jump or anything. I guess that's because I've been having such a hard time.

"I thought that two-and-two pitch was in and a little down. I guess in a way I shouldn't have taken it. Suppose he called it a strike? But you know, I've played against this guy [Jim Brewer] before. He's a left-hander, but I always hit him good. In '59 I was with Green Bay, he was with Burlington in the Three-I league. He's not a tough left-hander. He's easy to hit. He comes over the top so the ball doesn't come in on you.

"I figured he'd come with a fast ball because he doesn't have too much confidence in his curve and that's what he did. I've only hit two grand slams before, both in the minor leagues, and they were off infielders who came in to pitch. You know, wild games.

"It was the strangest feeling I've ever had. I've been down in the dumps the last couple of weeks and when I saw it go the only thing I said to myself was, 'About time.'

Leonard Shecter

I wasn't thinking of the crowd and how it would make them happy, only of myself.

"I've just been having a hard time. I read the newspapers. It's a lot harder to stay here than it is to get here. I'm one of those worriers. I think I've been lousy. I've been trying to figure a way to get out of it. I think I've found it. I was hitting off my front foot. It was anxiety, I guess. So I been getting jammed a lot. Every day I go through the same routine. I come out to the park and say I'll try this or I'll try that and I hope it works. But today I felt good after batting practice.

"Coming up this time I was so tired. I had three hits. It wasn't like I was oh for five and the pressure was on me. You can't do it every time. I guess I should feel like that every day. But I'm always thinking about something. I work for a brewery in Montreal. Maurice Richard is my boss. I ask him, 'Maurice, what are you thinking about when you come in to score a goal?' And he says, 'Nothing.' I guess I should be that way hitting.

"I'm a worrier. I worry like twenty-five other ballplayers on this club. I just have to look at my batting average [.208 going in, .222 coming out] and it hurts my stomach. I have a lot of pride. Not so much for myself. The people at home. I hate to be a lousy ballplayer.

"One of these days when I amount to something I'll probably be better for all this. I'll relax and enjoy people a little better. Baseball would be real good to me if I did well enough to satisfy the front office. It would make me a better person.

"I'd like to have people like me. But I don't know how to do it. I don't know how to get around it. I may not look it, but I need to be liked.

"I'm a worrier. When I hit the home run I looked over

Once Upon a Time . . .

at my wife. She was sitting next to the dugout. I been telling her every day to keep my bags packed."

Casey Stengel had said of Harkness in the spring, "Let me play him for a week and I'll get rid of him." The old man was wrong. Harkness lasted the season. He hit .211.

There was a point early in the season when the Mets had only two catchers, Norm Sherry, who was batting under .100, and Choo Choo Coleman who was batting barely over .200. This made Choo Choo a big man, which is what Casey Stengel wanted people to think. It's possible that he saw himself as a Svengali who would transform Choo Choo into another Yogi Berra. The old man always defended his little catcher. "They say he's not too smart," he'd grumble. "But I put the other fella in and the balls are hit over a building just the same." He would also point out, at every opportunity, that Choo Choo had great speed, and this, Roger Angell once wrote in the *New Yorker*, was "as necessary to a catcher as good handwriting." Choo Choo, Angell also wrote, "caught as though he were fighting a swarm of bees."

But the worst knock on Choo Choo was delivered by one Clarence Nottingham Churn III, a pitcher who played briefly for the Dodgers and the Pirates. He also had the good fortune to be on the same team with Choo Choo in Triple-A Spokane one year. And when someone asked him, "Who's the toughest guy in the league to pitch to," he answered, "Choo Choo Coleman."

After a while, Met fans became as famous as Met players. They were the objects of social evaluations. Did they want to lose? Were they losers themselves? An off-Broadway revue called, *Put It in Writing*, had a song in it which

Leonard Shecter

took the view that Met fans indeed were losers who wanted to lose more. Sung by actors who were supposed to be fans, the song went like this:

> That was quite an exhibition you gave the crowd today,
> Three triples and a home run and a snappy double play.
> You played it like a champion there isn't any doubt,
> Well, from now on, Buster, CUT IT OUT!
>
> On this here club we're happiest when other teams outscore us
> Frankly kid, the more we lose, the more the fans adore us.
>
> When you run for a ball run right into the stands
> Don't forget, you're a Met
> When a grounder arrives let it slip through your hands
> Don't forget, you're a Met
> When the ump says, "You're out!" never put up a fight
> Just turn and say politely, "Why you're perfectly right!"
> Playing Little League ball is what your contract demands
> Don't forget, you're a Met!

The fact was, though, that while Met fans loved the Mets when they lost, it was a love like that a mother bestows on a son who has just missed a scholarship. Better things had been expected.

Once Upon a Time . . .

The fans cheered the Mets on to win, not lose. They adored Ron Hunt because he got his uniform dirty, and at the slightest sign that a Met player was dogging it, they'd hold up signs that read: BOO!

"They're too much," Jimmy Piersall once said. "Do they go home and rehearse at night?"

It should be noted, too, that there was a different flavor to the crowds at the Polo Grounds than those that showed up later at suburban Shea Stadium. The fans were raunchier, somehow. They seemed to drink more beer and spill more of it on themselves and in the stands. They laughed a lot more, too, and seemed to have a better time—even when the Mets were losing.

The fans at Shea have a good time, too, these days. But winning seems more important to them. Maybe too important.

A story here about the quality of Met fans. This was while Marv Throneberry was still with the club. It was a rainy day and people were just goofing around in the clubhouse. Gil Hodges posed a riddle: A yacht has a ladder with rungs one foot apart. At low tide two rungs are in the water. At high tide, when the water rises three feet, how many rungs are in the water?

The whole thing was so simple-minded, I wrote a kidding item about it in the column I was doing for the *Post*, and secure in the knowledge that all readers of my pillar of erudition would know I didn't mean it, I offered "an autographed copy of Marv Throneberry" to anybody who answered the riddle correctly. Here's a sample of the huge mail response I got:

The answer is: Two rungs are in the water. I am

Leonard Shecter

wildly enthusiastic about receiving my copy of Marvelous Marv Throneberry.

Mark Chester

P.S. Please rush.

• • •

There will be two rungs below the water level. Please send my free autographed copy of Marvelous Marv Throneberry.

Alan Horwitz

P.S. What do I have to do to get a copy of Cliff Cook?

• • •

I do not know the answer to the question asked. But I would appreciate an autographed picture of Marv Throneberry.

Harvey Scheuer

• • •

Two rungs are in the water at high tide. Please send Throneberry.

Phillip Bustin

• • •

Two rungs. If you can't send Marvelous Marv I'll settle for Fabulous Faye [Marv's mediocre brother].

Gail Book

• • •

At high tide 5 (five) rungs are under water. Thank you.

R. Herman

• • •

Fans like that are hard to beat.

Once Upon a Time . . .

On July 7, with the Mets on a 10-game losing streak and his batting average at .190, Ed Kranepool was sent down to Buffalo. Larry Bearnarth, his roommate, explained: "I was fooled by him. I thought nothing could bother him. But he started getting very defensive when things got bad. Everything bothered him. He heard people yell at him and he couldn't ignore it. And he took to heart the little needling that all young players get."

More than that. One time Duke Snider tried to take him aside and give young Kranepool a batting tip. Kranepool refused to listen. Said the rookie to the gray, grizzled veteran, "You're not going that good yourself."

He wasn't all that tough, though. He blew a double play and a game one time for Bearnarth. The pitcher found him back in their room, bawling.

This Met losing streak was kept alive by hair-raising things like Big Donkey Thomas hitting into a 380-foot double play and Larry Burright backing up under a pop fly, standing there popping a fist into his glove, only to discover the ball thunking to the ground five feet away. It was continued amid definite word that Shea Stadium would not be ready this season and amid a heartbreaking losing streak for Roger Craig that had people showing up to work in the morning with boiled eyeballs. The toughest loss of all for Craig was his fourteenth in a row. He had the Phillies beaten 1–0 going into the ninth when he gave it away with two pitches—a double to Tony Gonzales, and a home run to Roy Siever, bang, bang—just like that. The next day Roger Craig received a letter from a lady fan: "I just put my head down on my arms and cried."

Craig never cried, at least not in public. He sat there

after every loss, a can of beer in his big hands, his elbows on his knees, sweat darkening his undershirt, and talked slowly, calmly, quietly. After this one he said: "I never had better stuff. I never had better control. I never had more confidence. And then one bad pitch . . ." He wasn't crying, but his Adam's apple bobbed a few times.

When Jimmy Piersall was released on July 22 he was batting .193. The fans had already turned their attention to Jesse Gonder, a catcher who swung a million-dollar stick and carried a five-and-dime glove. "UP YONDER WITH GONDER," a banner said. "NINTH PLACE OR BUST," read another. "BLESSED ARE THE METS, FOR THEY SHALL INHERIT THE PENNANT." The banners were great, the catching terrible.

There was this game the Mets lost in Pittsburgh because Gonder stood there and watched a ball thrown by Joe Christopher go all the way to the screen while two runners scurried around the bases and scored. It was the ninth inning and the Mets lost 2–1. Roger Craig wasn't even pitching.

Of course Gonder alone wasn't at fault. It all started with the Mets leading 1–0 in the ninth. Dick Schofield walked. Manny Mota dumped what should have been a single in front of Duke Carmel, a relatively recent Met acquisition. The first thing Carmel did was fumble the ball. Then he overran it. So Joe Christopher hustled over, picked up the ball and heaved it in the general direction of the infield. Now it was possible at this point to settle for runners on second and third. All Tim Harkness, at first, had to do was cut the ball off. Instead he sort of stood there, mouth open, like he was watching an X-rated

Once Upon a Time . . .

movie. Even so, disaster could have been averted if Galen Cisco, the pitcher, had been guarding the foul line as he should have been. Instead, he stood on the mound also watching the runners go round. It was like Saturday matinee at the circus. Finally, Gonder could have come up with the ball if he had hustled after it. Instead, he seemed nailed to the plate by the horror of it all.

"You ever see anything like that?" a reporter asked Casey Stengel.

"I seen everything," the old man said.

And Gonder? "Just one of those things," he said.

At one point in the season the Mets lost 29 of 31 games. Think about that. It's two wins in a month. And when Craig lost his seventeenth in a row on July 31 he admitted that he'd been praying during "The Star-Spangled Banner." "I don't pray for myself—not for help," Craig said. "I just ask Him to be part of the team." He had the right formula, just the wrong year.

Craig lost his eighteenth in a row (his record was 2–20) on August 4. This one went on a pickoff throw. Big Donkey Thomas was playing first base and holding a runner close, Craig kept tossing the ball over. After he felt he had sufficiently lulled the runner, Craig fired over with his best pickoff shot. Thomas let the ball roll clear back to the seats. It was the beginning of the end. The Mets lost 2–1.

"Should I have had it, Rodg?" asked a sad-eyed, contrite Thomas.

Craig didn't answer. He just shrugged his shoulders.

It was in this game, too, that Ed Kranepool, just back from Buffalo, got four hits and then, in the ninth, with the tying run on second, took a third called strike. The bat never left his shoulder. "That wasn't a strike," Kranepool said when he was questioned about it. "They wouldn't call Musial out on that pitch."

Galen Cisco had played for the two brightest managerial brains in sporting America—Woody Hayes at Ohio State and Casey Stengel with the Mets. So somebody asked him to compare the two. He thought for a while and said, "Woody's bigger."

Banner: "LET'S GO METS—KEEP MRS. PAYSON OUT OF DEBT."

On August 8 the Mets had put together a winning streak of two. "Amazin'," said Casey Stengel. "But I don't think we can catch the Dodgers—unless we play winter ball."

No doubt about it, the losing would get to Stengel from time to time. Someone once asked him if he ever chewed out his players in the dugout, which was something the Yankees used to complain about before the crusty old man was informed his services were no longer required over there. Of course the Mets were not the Yankees and no one knew it better than Stengel. So he said, "Nah, whaddaya want me to do, bite somebody?"

Then he sighed and added: "I wish they'd put in a lousy pitcher so he could win, 9–8."

When he actually got angry at his Mets Stengel would

Once Upon a Time...

call them "frauds." And the biggest fraud of all, in his book, was Craig Anderson, the pitcher. In 1962 Anderson compiled a 3-17 record with the Mets and a 5.35 ERA. In September of 1963 he was recalled from Buffalo to the Mets over Stengel's opposition. The kindly old manager couldn't wait to prove Anderson's worth. He put him into a game which the Mets were losing 5-0 and what followed was single, force, single, wild pitch, wild pitch, single, walk, force, single, and Casey Stengel clumping out to the mound with an ill-concealed smile on his face. Nothing he liked better than showing up a fraud.

After the game, lost by the Mets 9-0, somebody asked him if he learned anything about his Buffalo players.

The old man's eyes lit up in amusement. And he laughed.

Stengel never counted Roger Craig as a fraud, though. He respected the skinny pitcher and there was much empathy between them. The old man knew how it felt to be a winner and what it was like to lose by close scores. So after Craig had lost 18 in a row (three games by 1-0 scores and three by 2-1) Stengel tried a whommy—he got Craig to change his uniform number to 13. And by gosh, it worked. Craig beat the Cubs 7-3, on August 9, on a grand slam home run by Jim Hickman. "I think he kissed me," Hickman said.

This started Craig on a three-game winning streak and by the end of the season he had a record of 5-22. It could have been worse, but it's hard to imagine how.

When he was traded to the Cards over the winter, Craig said that despite what most people thought, it

Leonard Shecter

wasn't the losing of all those low-run games that bothered him most. The worst times, he said, especially during the losing streak, were when he pitched poorly. "Five or six times they got to me in the first five innings," Craig said. "That upset me more than losing 1–0. The other times at least I could say, 'Well, I didn't get racked.' "

It's odd, though, that there were Metsophiles who didn't appreciate Craig. ("He came to the end of the string with us," George Weiss said when he traded him.) They believed that Craig was a loser, and if he didn't lose 1–0 he'd find a way to lose 9–8. They pointed out that he had, after all, never won more than 11 games in his whole career. He pitched, they said, just well enough to lose.

To this Craig said, "I know there were guys on the club who won more games than I did. I don't know if it was luck or what. But I had a better earned-run average. And I don't consider myself a loser. I helped the Dodgers win two pennants.

"Another thing. The people who say I'm a loser," and there was a crackle to his voice now, "tell them I'll show them next year."

Alas, even this was not to be. Craig had a 7–9 record with St. Louis in 1964 and a 3.25 ERA. Still, the Cards won the pennant and Craig won a game in the World Series. After that he was traded to Cincinnati where he was 1–4 and to Philadelphia in '66 where he was 2–1. He is now a coach with the San Diego Padres and it is impossible to see him without thinking of him sitting on his stool, a can of beer in his hand, a sad look on his long thin face, and the weight of the world on his shoulders.

In the end, Craig can only be judged as a Met among Mets, loser among losers. It's even appropriate to recall at this point something he said in 1962 when Gil Hodges

Once Upon a Time . . .

was being given a night at the Polo Grounds. "Gil Hodges will never be a manager," Roger Craig said. "He doesn't want it. Being a manager means he'll have to talk to people at banquets and things like that. It's the only thing he really hates."

To the fans the Mets weren't just a baseball team anymore, they were like a bad cold. Once you had the Mets inside you all you could do was curl up with a good book and a bottle of whiskey and enjoy yourself. And every once in a while there would be a reward. Like in early September the Mets actually beat the Giants two in a row. This so upset Manager Alvin Dark that he kept the Giants after school for an hour-and-a-half practice. Stengel was delighted.

"They asked my permission," he said, "and I said they could have the field at six A.M. But then I figured it would stop all those nice fellows from going to church so I said they could do it now." He looked out of the window of his little office at the Giants working on the field and chuckled.

All season long the fans at the Polo Grounds had chanted "Let's Go Dook" at Duke Snider. On September 12 they gave him a night and a golf cart and an automobile and a trip to anywhere in the world for two. One of the wires to Snider that night read: "I never thought I'd live to see the day they would have a night for you in the Polo Grounds." It was signed Pee Wee Reese.

Snider was so overcome that he decided the only fitting thing he could do was hit a home run. "I went out there to hit one out," he said later. Of course he didn't. In fact he didn't get a hit and the Mets were shut out 6–0 by Juan Marichal. If you're a Met, that's as good a way to go as any.

September 15, 1963 was the Mets' first official Banner Day. In a burst of brilliant public relations, as uncommon to them as winning, the Mets front office gave its official sanction to a phenomenon it did not understand. It invited the fans to a banner competition. This has since become a yearly event, always well attended, always closely competed. Among the best that appeared that first Banner Day were:

KNOW WHY THE METS ARE SUCH GOOD LOSERS?
PRACTICE MAKES PERFECT

YOU MAY BE DOWN ON YOUR CANS
BUT YOU'RE FIRST WITH THE FANS

I PLEDGE ALLEGIANCE TO THE METS
OF THE NATIONAL BASEBALL LEAGUE
AND TO THE POLO GROUNDS FOR WHICH
IT STANDS, ONE TEAM UNDER CASEY,
INDIVISIBLE, WITH FUN AND EXCITEMENT
FOR ALL.

And this plaintive little one which won a plaintive little prize:

THIS SIGN IS IN FAVOR OF THE METS

When the parade of banners was over, the Mets dashed out on the field, each one of them carrying a large, printed letter. When they got themselves properly arranged and held them up, the letters spelled out, "TO THE MET FANS,

Once Upon a Time . . .

WE LOVE YOU TOO." And then Casey Stengel pranced out of the dugout carrying the final sign. It read "!".

It was a fine and touching thing loved by everyone except some of the ballplayers, who said, typically, "We're ballplayers, not sign carriers."

The way the schedule broke, the Mets played the last baseball game at the Polo Grounds on September 18. There were only 1,752 people who paid their way in to say good-bye. Another 271, most of whom didn't have to be there, came in on the cuff. Louie Kleppel was in the bleachers, of course, and he looked around the nearly empty ball park and said, "Not many really cared, did they?"

Louie Kleppel was wrong. Many cared. There are many who still do. The Polo Grounds, green and ugly, scrunched into Coogan's Bluff as though trying to hide its ugliness, was a place uncounted thousands of us remember going to as boys. We can still tingle with the excitement we felt as we came out of the subway. We recall the feeling of delicious hurry as we hiked across the bridge from the Bronx, from the monolithic Yankee Stadium, which never seemed so warm, so friendly, and so comfortably dilapidated as the Polo Grounds. On game days, the flags flew all around the top of the old ball park and from the bridge you could see them flapping contentedly. When you got close to the park there was the delicious odor of roasting peanuts and the cheerful whistling of the vendors' ovens. Inside, you were quickly caught up in this sense of intimacy with the players. Even if you sat in the outfield, you could at least see the expression on the fielder's face closest to you. You felt you could reach out and touch him. And it was something, in

Leonard Shecter

those days, to touch a major-league baseball player.

There's a housing project on the site of the Polo Grounds now, red brick and ugly. People don't pour out of the subway full of bustle and excitement there anymore. There are no flags, no peanut vendors. There is no Polo Grounds and we are all the poorer for it.

Of course, the Mets lost the last game played at the Polo Grounds. The Phillies beat them 5–1 and Craig Anderson was, fittingly enough, the losing pitcher. There were, naturally, jokes in the press box. When Ted Schreiber grounded into a double play with Bobby Wine playing short and Cookie Rojas playing second, it was "a play of Wine and Rojas." And there was laughter about all the losing records the Mets had set and the "negative statistics" which the club would never provide but which would be dug out gleefully by reporters anyway.

And some people pretended no feelings at all. "To hell with it," said Duke Snider. "This place messed up more good hitters than any park in history."

And Casey Stengel said: "Next year I'm going to pull my pitchers earlier, when they start to blow."

But there were people who walked out of the Polo Grounds with tears in their eyes, which is the way it should have been. At least someone cried when the Polo Grounds died.

Still, for others, for Met fans, it was less an ending than a beginning. And possibly they were thinking, as they left, of a banner which had touched thousands one losing day at the Polo Grounds. It said:

                WE SHALL OVERCOME

And now we have.

There was never a team like the old Mets and there

Once Upon a Time ...

will never be another. It was put together by a chain of incredible coincidences—the mendacity of National League clubowners who wanted to give up as few good players as possible in the expansion draft; the dogged, mistaken logic of George Weiss; the wildly improbable personality of Casey Stengel; the eccentrically shaped ball park itself. To have been there when these coincidences collided with such shattering hilarity was to have been someplace special indeed.

It is different now, obviously. Casey Stengel is gone. A pennant has been won, and a world championship. It is a glorious thing, and yet it is somehow sad. For what we feel for the Mets now will never be quite the same as what we felt for them in those first two years. We have tasted victory and we shall root not for survival, but for more victory. It was inevitable, we understand now, for this to happen; it's only that it happened so soon, so swiftly. Still, the Mets are still there (at slightly higher prices) and there is still much joy to take from them. We cannot be blamed, though, those of us who sit amidst the thundering crowd and quietly tell our young ones a tale that begins: "Once upon the Polo Grounds..."